KT-435-572

F**K YOU, PENGUIN

Hans Van Camp / Shutterstock Images LLC

F**K YOU, PENGUIN

TELLING CUTE ANIMALS WHAT'S WHAT

MATTHEW GASTEIER

HarperCollins*Publishers*

HarperCollins*Publishers*
77–85 Fulham Palace Road
Hammersmith, London W6 8JB
www.harpercollins.co.uk

First published by HarperCollins in 2009
2

Text © Matthew Glasteier 2009

Illustrations © Emily Flake

Matthew Glasteier asserts the moral right to be
identified as the author of this work

A catalogue record of this book is
available from the British Library

ISBN 978-0-00-732551-1

Printed and bound in Great Britain by
Martins the Printers, Berwick upon Tweed

All rights reserved. No part of this publication may be
reproduced, stored in a retrieval system, or transmitted,
in any form or by any means, electronic, mechanical,
photocopying, recording or otherwise, without the prior
written permission of the publishers.

Contents

Introduction

By the time you read this, I may have already saved the world. Actually, the mere fact that you purchased this book absolves you of all your sins, and you can basically do whatever you want for the rest of the year. Might I suggest drinking more and throwing your trash away less?*

Yes, you have become part of a great worldwide movement, a step towards stemming the tide of cute animals taking over our lives and our computers. Just in the past five years alone, cute animals have overtaken pornography as the number one thing clogging the Internet.

*** If you are reading this in the book store and you have no intention of paying for it, you are screwed, according to karma. I'm sorry, it's out of my control.**

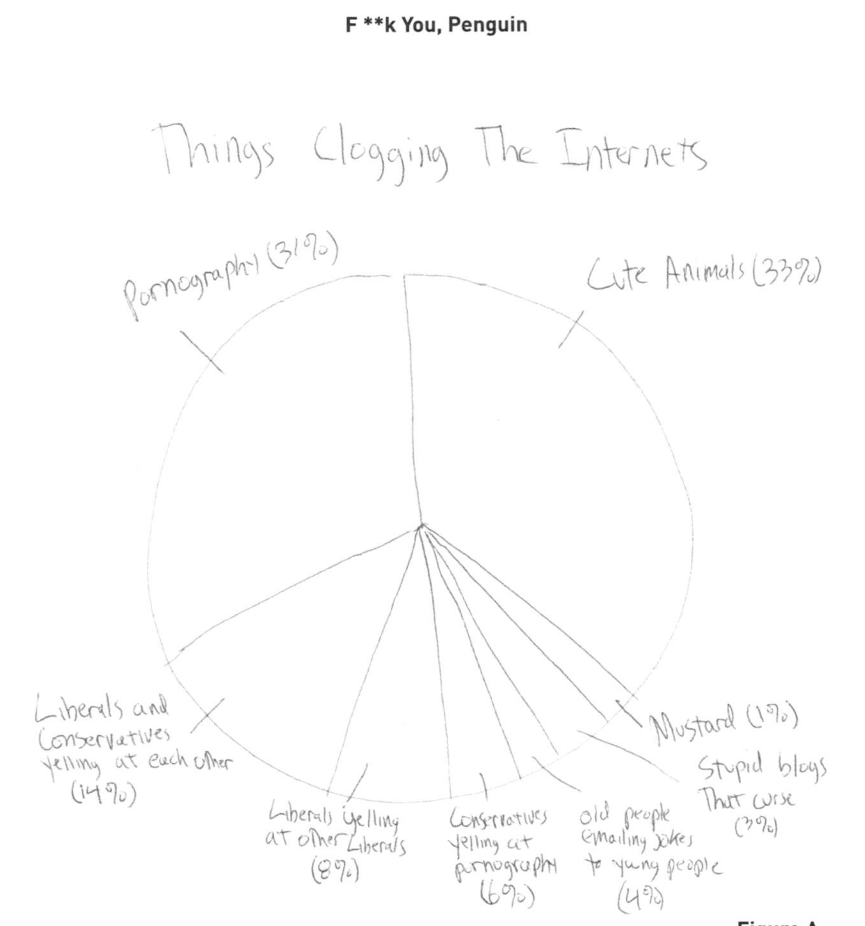

Figure A

Chart provided by J. Wass at The Fake Institute (TFI)

(See Figure A.) Do you realize what this means? I can't even shop for a daily calendar or watch *Animal Planet* during halftime of the Super Bowl without having to look at puppies and bunnies and kittens, completely out in the open for the most unsuspecting children to stumble upon, tainting their innocence for the rest of their lives.

That is, after all, why I started Fuck You, Penguin: for the children. I wasn't always this strong (thank you for noticing, by the way). I used to spend hours looking at pictures of cute animals. I ruined relationships. I stole from my friends to buy plush toys. I even got arrested one night trying to set myself on fire in the driveway of movie star Bart the Bear's Beverly Hills estate.

But my lowest point came a few months later. Desperate to get closer to my favourite animal, the elusive emperor penguin, I went on holiday to the Arctic. After spending months there searching for the animal, and getting frostbite on three separate fingers on four separate occasions, I discovered that penguins were rarely seen in the Arctic Circle. In reality, they spend their time in the more exclusive, penguin-only region of Antarctica.

*** Quite literally, as it was January in the Arctic and there was no sunlight.**

You can imagine my disappointment. But in that moment, one of the darkest I have experienced in my life*, I began to realize what effect this obsession was having on my life. I thought back to something an old friend had said: 'I can has cheezburger?' And I realized, *that makes no fucking sense.* If you are going to ask for a fucking cheeseburger, I thought to myself, the least you can do is spell it correctly, you stupid, stupid cat.

Suddenly, I knew what had to be done. These animals had got out of control. They were growing more confident with every passing day, as more people added them to their Facebook profiles and more grandmothers forwarded stories of the real-life Bambi and Thumper with notes attached like 'Smile! It makes your heart feel good!' (Oh, I'm sorry, Granny, are you a fucking doctor now?)

And above it all, there were the penguins. The penguins, with their Oscar, and their spin-off cartoon sell-out movie. The penguins, with their freeware computer operating system and their overpriced stuffed animals that I was forced to purchase (and that I do NOT still cuddle with). The penguins, the penguins, THE PENGUINS.

I quickly caught the first polar bear back to civilization, where I started what would be my lifelong passion (sorry, ladies), my gift to society (again, very sorry) and the greatest blog ever created: Fuck You, Penguin. The world hasn't been the same since.

And penguins? They know. They pretend they don't care, but I know they do. Every once in a while, I'll get a hit from Antarctica, or a remote area of Chile. They are keeping an eye on me, checking to see if this movement takes flight. Because if there's one thing penguins fear, it's flying. Let's make them afraid, people. Let's do it for our children and our children's children. And one day, together, we can look at a kitten cuddling with a parakeet and say, 'Enough!' And the kitten and parakeet will know exactly what they have done. And they will be ashamed. And all will be right with the world.

A helpful guide to placing *F**k You, Penguin* in the canon of Western civilization

To give you an idea of how important this book is, I've put together a modest collection of literature that has had a similar impact on humanity. I wouldn't presume to say that my book is anywhere near as good as these alltime classics, just that it is as important.

© iStockphoto.com

The Bible

By: God

Just as *F**k You, Penguin* has become the bible for people who want to put cute animals in their place, The Bible was, in some ways, a bible for many people in its own right. I suppose, if you really think about it, God in general has arguably had a larger impact on human history than I have, but just comparing what's on the written page, it's pretty much a draw.

That's not to say that there aren't some really great things about The Bible. In fact, I think The Bible is pretty similar to *F**k You, Penguin*, most notably in the second, more kid-friendly half, because Jesus never took any shit from penguins.

Jacket of THE JUNGLE by Upton Sinclair used by permission of Bantam Books, a division of Random House, Inc.

The Jungle

By: Upton Sinclair

This book is hugely influential in making high-school students really bored, but before that it was a big hit with people who wanted to eat food that didn't have the proletariat in it. Sinclair also wanted to make people think about the horrible oppression by the robber barons, and that's where it gets interesting because penguins are kind of the robber barons of the twenty-first century (except for the actual robber barons of the twenty-first century).

While I think *The Jungle* is pretty good, I think my book is a little bit more hard-hitting, without being so goddamned preachy. I actually originally wrote this book in the form of a novel, but then I realized that 'novelty' picture books sell much better, and I'm no fucking commie.

NOTE: This book should not be confused with *The Jungle Book*, which is pro-bear propaganda.

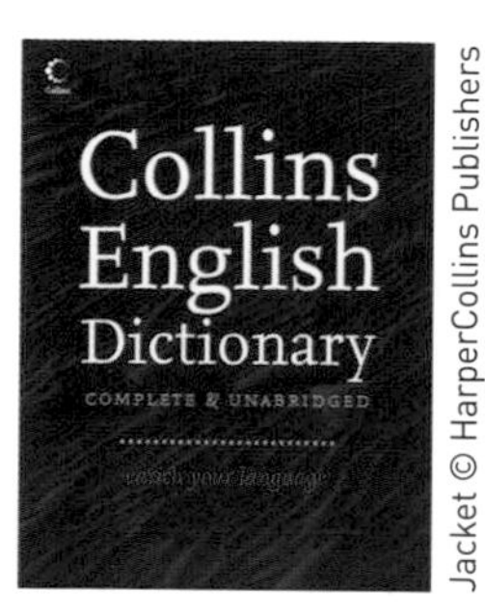

Jacket © HarperCollins Publishers

Collins English Dictionary: Complete and unabridged

By: People who don't use the word 'gotta'

Obviously, as a pure reference book, it's hard to beat the dictionary. But I think if you hold on to *F**k You, Penguin* for a little while, you'll start to see how often you come back to it. Is there anything more important than making sure these animals know their place? I would argue that even without the dictionary, this book would be quite effective as a deterrent for animals all over the world, since most cute animals don't even take the time to learn English in the first place.

I'm not going to pretend the dictionary doesn't come in handy, but you have to admit it's nice to have a book that doesn't require a Scrabble board in order to be useful.

Penguins

Public Enemy Number One

The 'it' animal of this first decade of the twenty-first century, the penguin has yet to use its fame and fortune for anything but its own self-interest, even accepting an outpouring of support for 'endangered' species of penguins. But if they are so endangered, how come there are so many pictures of them on my computer's hard drive? They even shamelessly accept fish in exchange for letting you spend a few minutes alone with one of them (Antarctica is the champagne room of the southern hemisphere). Thoughtlessly waddling into our hearts with *March of the Penguins*, these birds didn't even feel it was necessary to appear in person for their cash-in films *Happy Feet* and *Surf's Up*, replacing themselves with cartoon imitations. Despite these half-hearted efforts, they have been able to get away with the equivalent of genocide on our psyches, and it's time they were stopped, International Criminal Court-style.

What follows is a detailed deconstruction of the ways in which penguins can ruin your day. DON'T LET THEM WIN. Together, we can stop this threat, and take back our lives from these overdressed con artists.

Penguins think they are so fucking great

Bryan Lintott / Shutterstock Images LLC

The worst part of all this attention on penguins is how much it has inflated their egos. This cocky bastard thinks he's Leo fucking DiCaprio on the bow of the *Titanic*, and while penguins can't talk (or, more likely, they think humans are beneath their talking abilities), he's basically saying 'I'm king of the world' with his body language.

Well, I've got news for you, Penguin. Just because you have tiny little flightless penguin wings that you are spreading like you want to give me a big bear hug and I can see your cute little penguin feet peeking out from under your penguin belly and you are an emperor penguin which is like a king does NOT mean that you are the king of the world, jerk. IN FACT, YOU ARE JUST A PENGUIN. It may be your world, now, Penguin, but I'm on to you. Watch your adorable fucking back.

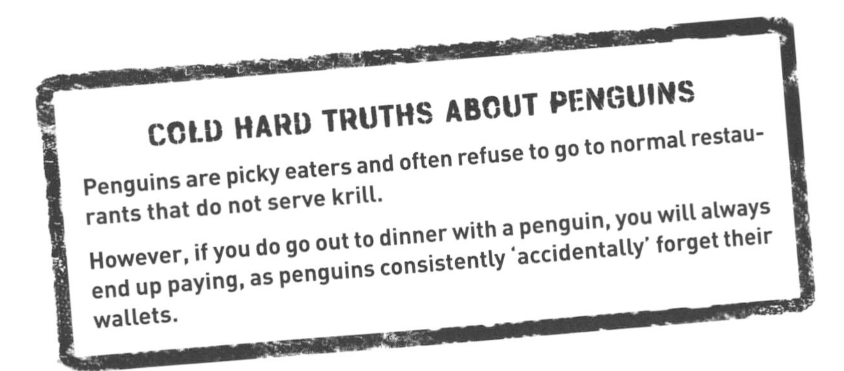

How are you still cute?

Brian L. Lambert / Shutterstock Images LLC

Penguins are into the thrills in life, so they play a lot of games like competing to see how batshit crazy they can look and still come off like a kitten in a fucking basket. This rock-hopping asshole went straight for the *Looney Tunes*-style crazy eyes, which go disgustingly great with the Mardi Gras feathers that come standard on one of these motherfuckers.

But, of course, that all wasn't good enough, was it, Penguin? So you gave me a smile that says, 'First I'm going to pick your child up from day care, and then I'm going to have sex with your wife before we all go out for a nice family dinner at the local Chili's.' And you still have the GODDAMNED NERVE to be cute. In *MY* GODDAMNED BOOK. Well, guess what, Penguin? I hate the player, *and* I hate the game. So get out of my face.

We are slaves to the penguins, people

AP Photo / Eric Risberg

This penguin was going bald, so he wasn't able to stay warm in the water, since penguins are too vain to get fatter and let their blubber keep them warm. So when Pierre over here (actual goddamned name) couldn't grow his own feathers, what did we do? WE GAVE HIM A WET SUIT TO KEEP HIM WARM. Now look at him, smirking away as he is lowered back down to show off his gear to his friends, like he did anything to deserve it.

Why are we such chumps, people? These penguins don't care about us, all they do is waddle around and have babies – adorable, smug little babies. And yet we put wet suits on them, and as if that's not enough, WE THEN WRITE NEWS ARTICLES ABOUT HOW CUTE THEY LOOK IN THE WET SUITS WE PUT THEM IN. Do you not see the vicious circle here, people? We will be free of the penguins only when we stop allowing them to have this power over us. Let's let Pierre buy his own wet suit. Then we'll see how cute it is when a bald penguin has to wait tables for a living.

Actually, that *would* be pretty cute ... Just give him the damn wet suit.

This doesn't concern you, Weddell Seal

Bryan Lintott / Shutterstock Images LLC

Hey, buddy, can you get the fuck out of my way? I'm trying to talk to the penguins, here. I know this is normally the part of the nature documentaries where you come in and get to be the bad guy because you run after the penguins and everyone boos. But guess what, asshole? NOT EVERYTHING IS ABOUT YOU, WEDDELL SEAL. You probably think we're going to be friends because I hate penguins, but all you do is drum up sympathy for the bastards, so you need to go back to squid and fish and let me handle the birds.

What are you so desperate for, anyway? You've got fat folds, short arms, a pudgy nose and a perpetual frown. YOU ARE A VORTEX OF CUTE. Pretty sad, Weddell Seal.

COLD HARD TRUTHS ABOUT PENGUINS

Penguins take it personally that so many of their kind are eaten by Weddell Seals. So when a seal is courting a special lady seal, a penguin will often come up and say something along the lines of 'Hey, how's the girlfriend, is she out of town?' just to make things difficult for the seal.

This would be totally understandable, except that when krill do the same thing to penguins, the penguins think it's a dick move.

Walk like a normal person, asshole

vulnificans / Shutterstock Images LLC

I don't know if you are making fun of people in double leg casts or if you are just trying to put me into a coma as you waddle into my heart, Penguin. But unless you are not at all trying to get where you are going, that is the dumbest way to walk that I can possibly imagine. FRONT TO BACK, NOT SIDE TO SIDE, MORON. What makes it so depressing is that you know damn well what you are doing. It's not like walking was just invented, *it's been around for years*. Well, I don't know who you think you are, Penguin, but it's time you learned how to get around properly. If you start walking the right way now, who knows? Maybe ten, twenty generations down the line, your legs will come back, and then you won't have to waddle around like some pathetic loser that can't even get away from a seal.

So start working it, Penguin. And if I catch you taking the easy way out by sliding on your belly, you are going to be in serious, serious trouble.

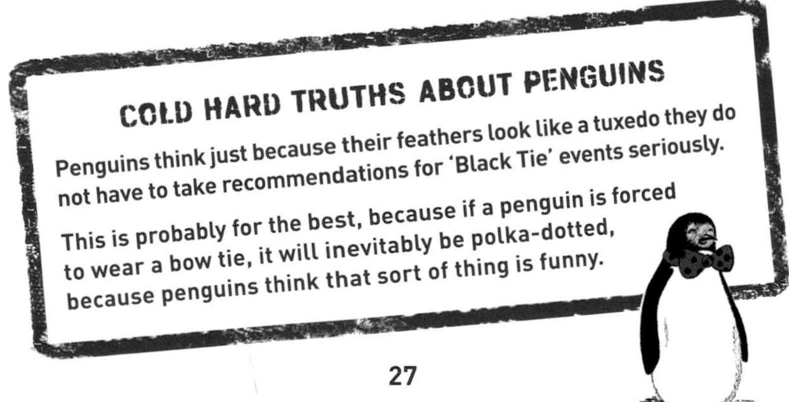

What did I just fucking say?

Rich Lindie / Shutterstock Images LLC

Are you kidding me, Penguin? Did you even read the last page, or are you just browsing here? YOU REALIZE THIS MEANS WAR, RIGHT, PENGUIN? Don't even look at me like that. You are sliding on your fat belly because your feet can't get around it to walk; meanwhile your wings are hanging in the air like the useless undeveloped appendages that they are (have you ever heard of toning, Penguin?), and you have the balls to be proud of yourself for defying me?

I've just about had it up to here with you penguins. You know, you waddle and slide, you flap your wings and hop on rocks, you don't get out of my dreams and into my car ... The whole thing is a fucking disaster. I can't even take this anymore; let's find some animals who are actually willing to face what they've done.

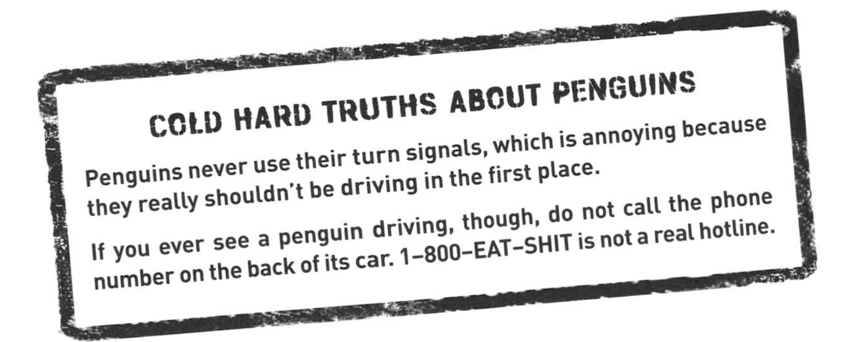

Domestic Terrorists

There is a threat perhaps even more terrifying than penguins. Not because they are bigger assholes than penguins, that would be impossible. It's because, unlike penguins, these jerks are in our very own homes.

Let me lay out a scenario for you. I come over to your house. You feed me, give me a place to sleep, scratch me behind my ears, and even take pictures of me and send them in to blogs so I can become world famous. And what do I do in exchange? I lie on my back and show you my furry belly, lick my paws, play with yarn, and am fascinated by plastic balls and the doorbell. Not cool, right?

Well, this is exactly what millions of people around the world have to put up with every day of their lives. Cats, dogs, and various other animals know that with one turn of the head or one cleverly placed paw, they could have us literally on our hands and knees to cater to their every whim. It's time to stand up to this home-grown threat, and say, 'NO, GINGER,' or whatever. Not that I have a Pomeranian named Ginger. I just mean in general.

Puppies always leave

Photograph by Claire A. Bartholome 2008.

This is a puppy I briefly housed at Fuck You, Penguin headquarters. Her name was Lexington, she peed on my bed, chewed a hole in my shower curtain, and licked my face when I wasn't looking. I loved her so.

But then she left me when her old family came back from vacation. And that's fine. Because you know what, Puppy? I have met another puppy since you've been gone. Actually, I've met a large number of puppies. And I've played with all of them. Sometimes more than one at the same time. In fact, just the other day I was cuddling with a puppy and thinking, 'This is so much better than that time I was cuddling with Lexi. Thank goodness she gave me back my freedom.'

I've moved on, Puppy. I've grown. I'm no longer that same inexperienced puppysitter you met on that warm August day. So don't come crawling back to me, Puppy. Don't even fucking think about it. Unless you want to. Then I'm sure we can work something out.

TRY THIS AT HOME

Dogs respond remarkably well to attempts to make them jealous. Next time you are feeling like your dog thinks it could do better, pretend to call other dogs on the telephone and say things like 'Oh, you are so silly!' and make plans to grab a bite. Then sit back and enjoy the affection.

What a couple of loser LOLcat wannabes

© John Seabury

I don't get it, Jack and Pepper, what's wrong with the normal life you lead? I'm sure you have a very nice family. They gave you a deck to hang out on, they even bought you collars, which I bet you didn't even offer to pay for, since cats are such cheap assholes.

So why do you have to try to make the big time with your desperate attempt at a LOLcat? I know what you are thinking, Pepper, I can see it in your eyes: 'All we have to do is look really evil like we are planning to kill the person who took the photo, and we'll be all over the Internet! We might even get on *Oprah*!' (Cats love *Oprah*.) Well guess what, Jack and Pepper (if those are even your real names and not some stage names you made up because Shlomo and Itzhak sounded too ethnic), I GOT TO YOU FIRST. So don't even think about adding giant misspelled words to this image, cats. Your fifteen minutes are up before they even began. Now go back to sleeping all day and licking your fur like normal, non-famous cats.

TRY THIS AT HOME

While they might not know it, what cats really like in life is structure. Try scheduling a busy day for your cat, with activities like karate and clarinet practice (or another woodwind). By the time your cat gets home, it will be so tired that all it will do is sleep and you will be able to get some much-needed rest.

You are a fucking mess

A.J. Maher

Are you kidding me, Dule? You have snow all over your face now. YOU LOOK LIKE A COKEHEAD IN HIS ROCK-BOTTOM MOMENT. I'm not even sure what made you think eating the snow was a good idea, seeing as how I just watched you peeing in the snow like five minutes ago, you dirty son of a bitch. You can do all the tail wagging you want, and standing by a barn like you are in an idealized childhood memory will get you only so far. At some point, you need to start acting like a grown-up and grooming yourself properly. You think chicks are going to respond to the shaggy look, Dule? 'Cause I've seen your type, and trolling at the local commune is not going to work.

And, I mean, yeah, you can still sleep in bed with me, but from now on you can only lick my face after I've eaten dinner.

TRY THIS AT HOME

Dogs can actually talk, but they know it would change the whole dynamic in their relationship with humans if they let on. The best way to convince your dog to talk to you is to start up a conversation about obscure nineteenth-century Russian poetry and misquote various verses. Your dog will be unable to resist correcting you.

Silly cat, ennui is for humans!

Rachel Otty

Sassafras, I asked you to put the dishes away, not sit by the window and contemplate the meaning of life. You've been moping around the house for the last, oh, FIVE YEARS, questioning the purpose of it all. Guess what, Sassafras? I would have gotten Plato to use the litter box if I had wanted a fucking philosopher for a pet.

There are three things I ask of you, Sassafras. One is to have cute patches of white fur in just the right spots. Two is to lick your paws when they need cleaning, or when there isn't anything on TV. And three is to LIVE EACH DAY LIKE IT MATTERS. Joie de vivre, Sassafras, joie de fucking vivre.

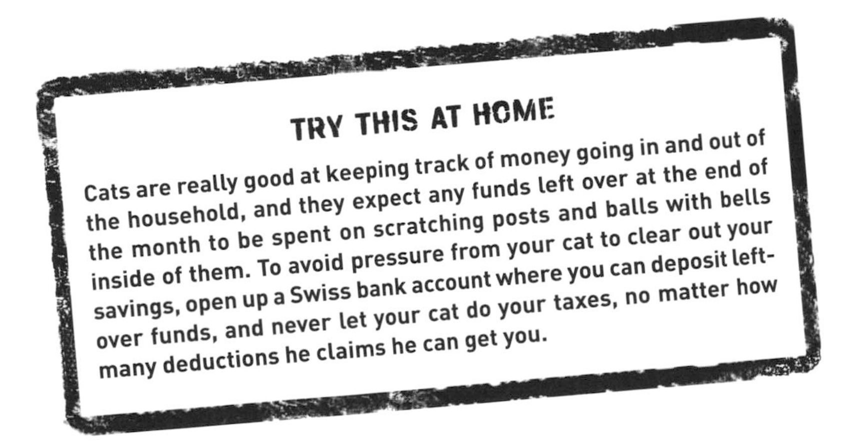

TRY THIS AT HOME

Cats are really good at keeping track of money going in and out of the household, and they expect any funds left over at the end of the month to be spent on scratching posts and balls with bells inside of them. To avoid pressure from your cat to clear out your savings, open up a Swiss bank account where you can deposit left-over funds, and never let your cat do your taxes, no matter how many deductions he claims he can get you.

Is a cookie really worth all this?

Kem B. Sypher

After returning from the hospital, Fuck You, Penguin confronts The Cookie Bunny ...

You know, Desdemona, I wasn't going to eat all of those cookies. If you had just asked me, I would have given you one. In fact, you could even have taken it without asking, and then gone on your way. But, no, you had to turn to me and look like you were caught in the act in a way that basically turned my insides to mush. You couldn't just be a bunny that took a cookie, Desdemona, no. YOU had to be The Cookie Bunny.

Now your face has been plastered all over the Internet, and I spend hours wandering the streets mumbling 'Cookie Bunny' to strangers. WHAT HAVE YOU DONE TO OUR RELATIONSHIP, COOKIE BUNNY? I thought we had something special. Instead, you were just another bunny, waiting for her moment in the sun. But I'm not your stepping-stone, Cookie Bunny. So I hope you enjoyed that cookie. Because from now on, I'm only making cupcakes.

TRY THIS AT HOME

Rabbits love to alphabetize things, so if you are worried about your rabbit being bored while you are at work, take out your CD/DVD/book collection and spread it all over the floor. By the time you get home, you will have a perfectly organized library and a happy bunny.

Spoiled dogs always expect more

Deena Lang

Oh, I'm sorry, Kona. I know you wanted a chocolate cupcake, but this was all I could get at the last minute, and anyway you happen to be a dog and CHOCOLATE KILLS DOGS. I'm just at a loss as to why you are making that face at the moment, and, no, it is not making me want to hold you in my arms and rock you back and forth, telling you everything is going to be okay.

Do you even see how good you have it, Kona? We got you a cupcake with a candle on it. We got you a happy birthday hat. We even let you sit on the furniture for your special day. And now you won't even eat the damn cake. Do you know that there are starving dogs in Africa that would be thrilled to have a cupcake? Look, Kona, I'm not mad. I'm just disappointed. Now eat your cupcake and go to your room and think about what you've done.

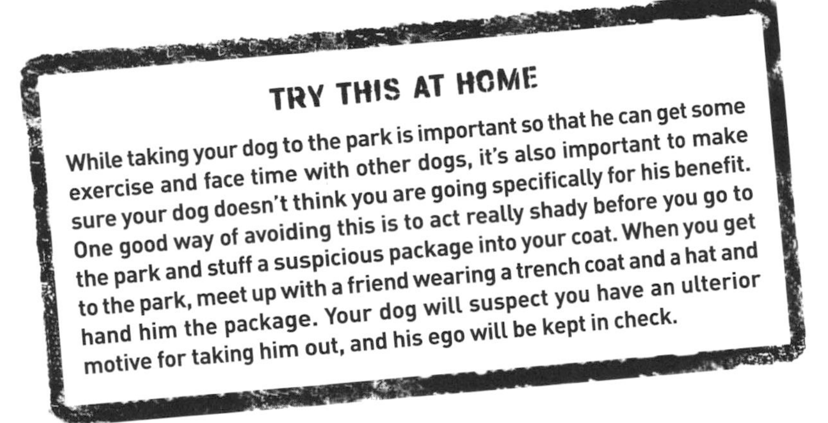

Would you like another pillow, sire?

Paul Sweedlund

Hey. Gomez. I didn't realize you were just going to have a relaxing day where you were being waited on hand and foot. Just because I came over and tucked you in doesn't mean I'm going to make up a tray of tuna fish for you when you wake up. What the fuck do you think you are doing cuddling up in my bed, anyway? MY BED IS NO PLACE FOR YOUR MOMENTS OF ADORABLE SERENITY. I'm going to have to wash my sheets, Gomez. Thanks a lot.

Well, Gomez, I'm off to work, the place where I make all of the money I spend on things like cat food, balls with bells inside them and making sure that you have a window you can stare out of all day long. But if you wake up from your little catnap and you need anything, PLEASE DON'T HESITATE TO NOT CALL.

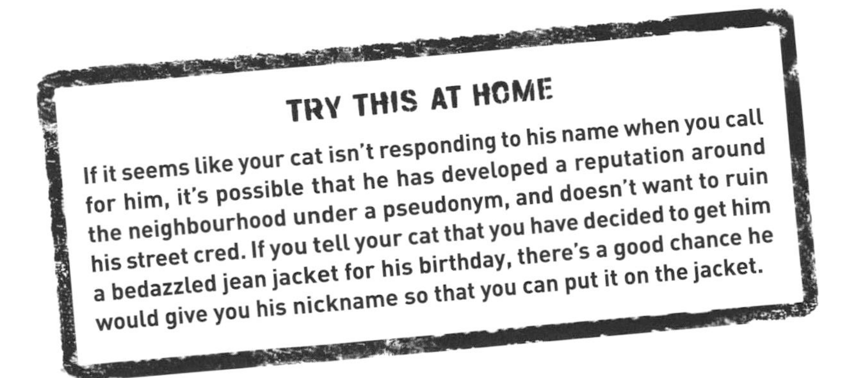

WARNING:
Dogs are big-time fakers

Joy Zaczyk

A lot of times being an awesome dog that gets to hang out and be loved all day isn't good enough for the greedy, self-centred bastards we let into our homes and hearts. So when you aren't looking, they'll run out into the street and lie down and start to cry. When you come over, they'll be like, 'Argh, I think it's busted. Darn guy came out of nowhere!' Then they'll get up and hop around for a little while, mumbling, 'Yeah, I definitely think there's something wrong with it.' One bribed veterinarian later and they are hopping around in their doggy cast, basically sending every person who sees them into epileptic shock from the tragic cuteness of it all.

Wilbur (opposite) is a perfect example. Instead of being content to be an ENGLISH FUCKING SHEEPDOG, THE SHAGGIEST DOG THERE IS, Wilbur had to up the ante and get a cast, which he convinced the vet assistant to customize with an 'ouch' message and even a heart. A goddamned pink heart. So next time your dog 'breaks his leg', get him the cast, put the 'ouch' message on it, make up his bed, tell him you love him and then make sure he knows if he pulls this shit ever again, he's out on the street.

TRY THIS AT HOME

It isn't easy to prevent your dog from drinking out of the toilet – sometimes you just forget to put the seat down. A little-known fact is that dogs hate merlot, and simply adding a glass of the wine to your toilet water after every use will have them reaching for their water bowl in no time.

You haven't thought this through

Lauren Billings

Oh, man, I am thirsty. Let's see what's in the fridge. We've got orange juice, purple stuff, a cat – WHAT THE FUCK?

Anton, I realize you are at your cutest when placed in unusual situations, but do you really think anything about this is appropriate? First of all, it's very cold in there, and while it might seem like you can eat anything you want, you lack most of the motor skills required to open containers. And I know I've said I wanted to eat you up in the past, but, Anton, that was a figure of speech. So, please, stop getting in the refrigerator, sleeping in small bowls and dressing up like Batman on Halloween. JUST BECAUSE I MAKE YOU DO SOMETHING DOESN'T MAKE IT OKAY. Next time you decide to ruin my day, I want you to think, 'Why am I doing this? And is it really worth the pain and suffering?'

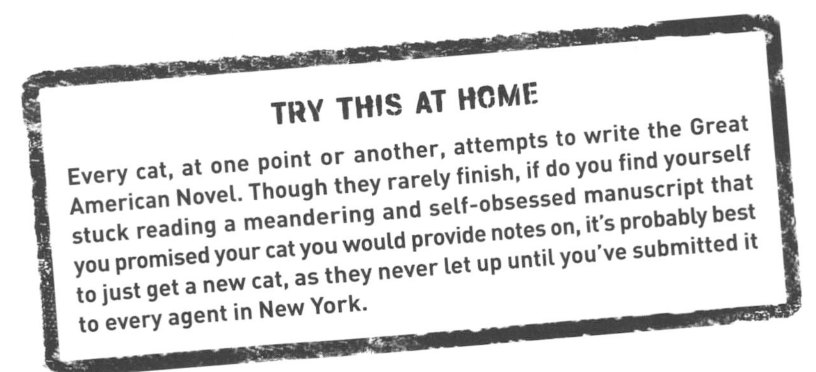

Rats are an unstoppable killing force

Pakhnyushcha / Shutterstock Images LLC

Rats are supposed to be terrifying, with their beady little eyes and their presumed guilt regarding the whole 'Bubonic Plague' thing. But lately, they've been acting like they are guinea pigs or something, wiggling their noses and starring in Pixar movies. It's all gone to their heads, and now they think they should be able to do whatever they want, no matter the consequences to my email inbox.

So I know what I said earlier, Algernon, but there is no way I can let you out of that cage. We both know what would happen if you were allowed to roam free. You would wave your little rat paws and your tiny rat nose around and take over the entire house with your cuteness. I can't believe you are even thinking about giving me that look right now. I know you are angry at me. I don't blame you. But the truth is, Algernon, despite all your rage, you are still just a rat in a cage. Deal with it.

TRY THIS AT HOME

Rats are hypersensitive about their reputation, so it's best to avoid talking about the negative aspects of the public perception of rats in front of your pet. To boost your pet's personal image, consider giving it a tour through rat history, chronicling the accomplishments of the species through time. Avoid giving him homework, though, as rats will eat any handouts you provide.

I happen to know for a fact that you can't use that thing

Denise Martinez Alanis

Okay, Roger, I realize that you are sitting in the chair and you have the laptop pulled up like you are typing away. Good fucking job. I'm sure you think I am going to be SUPER-IMPRESSED by the scene you have set. But guess what, Roger? I know dogs can't use computers. Apart from the obvious thumb problem, dogs are less technologically advanced than old people, and since my grandmother doesn't know how to use a computer, there's no way you can. Unless this is all one big joke, designed to make me think my grandmother is stupid. WHICH ONE IS IT, Roger? WAS THIS ALL A RUSE DESIGNED TO GET A TREAT, OR DO YOU HATE MY GRANDMOTHER? Your game has been revealed either way, my friend. Now log out of my Salon.com account. No one cares what you think about the pros and cons of Western European-style public insurance systems and their impact on labour-market productivity.

TRY THIS AT HOME

Dogs are obsessed with digital video recorders because they are always sleeping during their favourite shows. However, it is best to have them use a separate DVR, as they almost never get around to watching anything, and even when they do, they never delete it.

Plotting cats think world domination is adorable

Crystal McKay

Okay, Kitty Cat Feline, pretty sure you are just a cat. I realize you've been worshipped for thousands of years, and being on a beaded pillow reminds you of the empire you once lorded over, but I also realize that you just spent the last twenty minutes staring at a string that was hanging from the ceiling fan. Basically, your best years are behind you.

And yet ...

What is it about you that still terrifies me? I think it's your quiet confidence, your paw waiting to snatch up the last best hope for humanity, and the fact that I can't help but want to come over there and rub you behind your ears until you start to purr. Okay, Kitty, you can have the nuclear codes, BUT USE THEM ONLY AS A LAST RESORT.

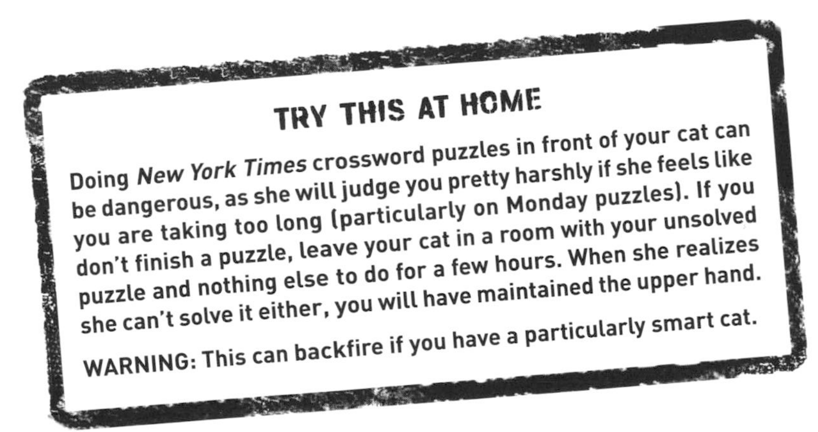

TRY THIS AT HOME

Doing *New York Times* crossword puzzles in front of your cat can be dangerous, as she will judge you pretty harshly if she feels like you are taking too long (particularly on Monday puzzles). If you don't finish a puzzle, leave your cat in a room with your unsolved puzzle and nothing else to do for a few hours. When she realizes she can't solve it either, you will have maintained the upper hand.

WARNING: This can backfire if you have a particularly smart cat.

Puppies love to remind you how small they are

Rebekah Winkler

Linus, get the hell away from that foot. Don't you know what you are doing to me? It's bad enough you will grow up to be a pudgy, drooling, underbite-sporting eighth wonder of the world. You also have to combine size comparisons with napping? Wake up and don't go near sneakers ever again, they can't possibly be small enough for you to sit next to them without reducing me to a babbling pile of affection.

Puppies are THE WORST. They expect you to let them get away with waking up and screaming through the night, peeing on the floor and chewing on everything, including your face. And what is their plan for getting away with all of that? Licking your face, waddling around and generally being very small. Well, guess what, Linus? It's only going to work on me ninety-five per cent of the time, SO YOU BETTER WATCH OUT.

Take the broccoli.
Leave my dignity

Mayuko Chrenka

Exhibit A

sngck / iStockphoto LP

Why, Kuma, why? I am but one poor soul, trying to make my way in the world. I do what every decent citizen is supposed to do. I call my grandmother on her birthday. I recycle whenever there is a recycling bin on my side of the room. For a living, I run a modest blog, where every morning I get up and try to give a little back to the world.

So why do you have to be such a soul-crushing asshole? It's just broccoli, Kuma, I'm not really sure why you are all 'Broccoli?! Wow, I never expected broccoli!' Everyone knows hamsters love broccoli before they can even see it (see Exhibit A). You are not fooling anyone. So my only guess as to why you are making that face is that you are actively trying to destroy me. Well, fuck you, Kuma. Because I've got the broccoli now. Or something. Shut up.

Please just go.

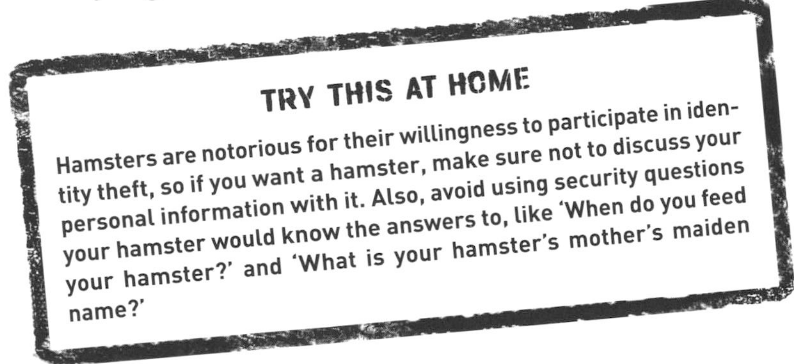

We. Are. Fucked.

Zach Walker

Oh, Jesus Christ, the horror, THE HORROR. How am I supposed to go on living my life knowing that kittens and bunnies can form like Voltron over a plate of chard? ONE AT A TIME, ASSHOLES. I ONLY HAVE ONE SET OF EYES – I CAN'T AFFORD TO HAVE THEM EXPLODE. What do you think you're doing, anyway? If *Lady and the Tramp* taught me anything, it's that traditional stringy food sharing is between a dog and another dog, none of this immoral kitten-on-bunny action.

Fortunately, there is a lesson that comes out of such a tragedy. You see, what we are dealing with here is a pre-kitten-and-bunny-eating-together mentality. We live in dangerous times, people. We can no longer afford to be naïve enough to think we can put out leafy greens and get away with it. Because if a kitten will team up with a bunny, then maybe a puppy will team up with a koala. Maybe a penguin will join forces with a camel. We need to stay strong, hold on to our produce, and spread rumours about how kittens are anticarrot.

TRY THIS AT HOME

If you own more than one species of animal, it is important to avoid establishing a democratic precedent that consists of 'one species, one vote' because animals will often caucus with each other, even if they come from traditionally antagonistic species like dogs and cats, in order to overpower the humans in the house. One wrong step and you could be sleeping outside.

Cute Animals At Large

It's not just the animals we interact with on a daily basis that need to answer for their behaviour. Because they get less attention than their counterparts on the inside, animals at large often work even harder to ruin your day. The most important thing to do when confronted with an animal at the zoo or running around the forest like it's the fucking Lion King is to stay calm and focus on letting it know that what it is doing is not cool.

Remember: Animals often have never been confronted about their behaviour, so these mini-interventions will be real eye-opening experiences for them. Hopefully, if they are mature and self-reflective enough, they'll really think about what got them to this point in life and start taking the first steps toward changing for the better.

Moose are the biggest dorks ever

© Robert Y. Ono / Corbis

Obviously, Moose, you don't have a mirror to practise your smile, because you seriously look like a total vagina right now. You are very lucky that moose do not have to go to school, since you would get your ass kicked, like, every day. And what kind of wild animal smiles at a camera? You are supposed to be a badass that roams the forest beating up other moose and cars that look at you funny, not Cindy fucking Crawford. Man up, Moose.

Just say no to kangaroos

Nick Biemans / Shutterstock Images LLC

Oh, I get it, Kangaroo. You're just hanging out, right? I bet if I asked you what you were doing, you would probably say you were 'chillaxin'' or something. You probably think you look pretty cool, but I know better, Kangaroo, because YOU ARE AS HIGH AS A KITE RIGHT NOW.

Kangaroo, did you ever stop to think about the kids? Do you ever think about anyone other than yourself, and perhaps Mallomars? No, you fucking don't. So fuck you, Kangaroo. You ought to be ashamed of yourself.

Endangered + Cute = Entitled

Tamir Niv / Shutterstock Images LLC

What have you done to survive today, Panda?

Oh, that's right.

Nothing.

All you do is sit there on your FAT PANDA ASS and eat bamboo all day. I bet you've eaten something ridiculous like twenty-five pounds of bamboo today, you fat bastard. You really have it made, don't you? You hang out all day, do nothing, and all you have to do is sit there and produce your furry panda belly like a son of a bitch and everyone is supposed to go crazy. Well, it's not going to work on me, Panda. I AM ON TO YOUR BELLY-RELATED GAMES. Your plot is starting to unravel, Panda. I wouldn't be surprised if by the time there are a couple billion of you guys, humans start making you fend for yourself. So enjoy it while it lasts, Panda, because once you mooches are able to thrive and roam free in your natural habitat, WE'RE KICKING YOU OUT OF OUR RESERVES, ASSHOLE.

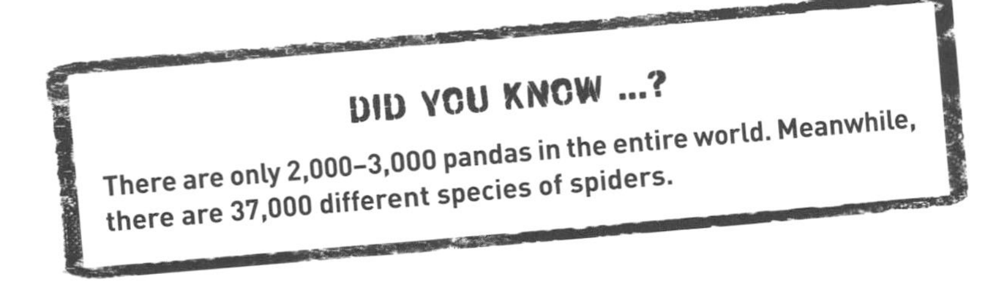

Laziest. Animal. Ever.

Alvaro Pantoja / Shutterstock Images LLC

Sloth, get off your fucking ass and get down out of that tree. I don't care if it is practically impossible for you to walk on the ground, you've been sleeping for nearly a full day now and you promised you would start looking for a job this morning. WELL, IT'S ALMOST TWO IN THE FUCKING AFTERNOON. And have you taken a shower recently? Your hair looks like it is literally made out of straw.

Goddamn, Sloth, you are the most appropriately named little fucker of all time.

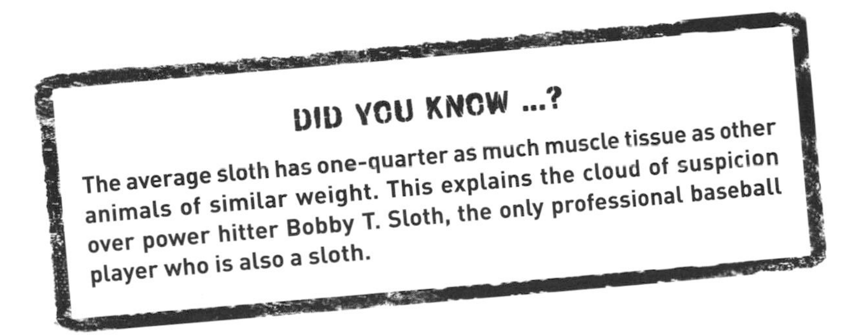

DID YOU KNOW ...?

The average sloth has one-quarter as much muscle tissue as other animals of similar weight. This explains the cloud of suspicion over power hitter Bobby T. Sloth, the only professional baseball player who is also a sloth.

Chipmunks: What are they hiding?

Jon R. Vermilye / Lakeshoreimages.com

What is going on inside those cheeks, Chipmunk? I know you've got something in there, because I KNOW you aren't doing a Marlon Brando impression. YOU DON'T EVEN KNOW WHO MARLON BRANDO IS BECAUSE YOU ARE JUST A FUCKING CHIPMUNK. And close your mouth while you are eating – no one wants to see your chewed-up whatever. Jesus Christ, Chipmunk. Manners.

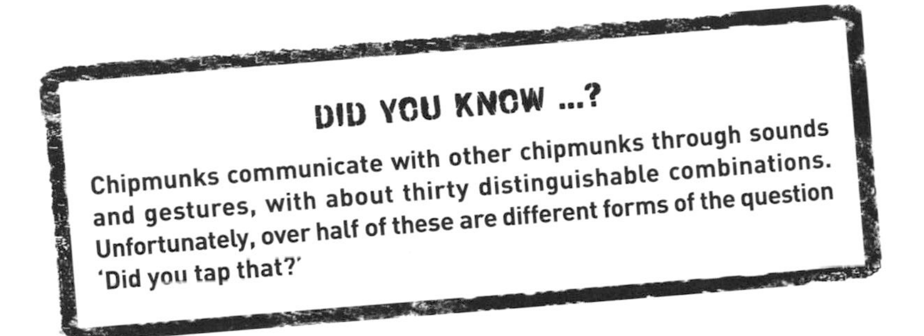

DID YOU KNOW …?

Chipmunks communicate with other chipmunks through sounds and gestures, with about thirty distinguishable combinations. Unfortunately, over half of these are different forms of the question 'Did you tap that?'

Are you fucking kidding me, Tamarin?

Luiz Claudio Marigo

What are you, in the witness protection programme? Or is that supposed to be ironic and you actually hate beards? Honestly, Tamarin, I think it's time to move on to a style that says something other than 'I'm a really big fan of the TV show *Kung Fu*'. And the tail, GOOD FUCKING GOD, MONKEY. There's no excuse for keeping yourself in such shoddy condition. ARE YOU A FUCKING CLEVELAND BROWNS FAN? I'm sure you've gotten away with a lot up to this point in your life because you are a monkey, and the more you look like an old man, the more attention you get. But it's time to grow up, Tamarin. Take some responsibility for your actions.

DID YOU KNOW ...?

The emperor tamarin is named after the German emperor Wilhelm II because the man who named it said the monkey looked like Wilhelm. Coincidentally, that person also has a tamarin named after him: the 'No-Head Hans' tamarin.

Self-Satisfied Lambs

© Caroline Rivard

Lamb, you think you're so fucking great because your head is a different colour than your body. Just being born in a barn doesn't make you the second coming of Jesus. IT'S JUST THE SUN, LAMB. ANYONE CAN LIE IN IT. What makes you so special? Fucking NOTHING, that's what, Lamb. All you do is prance around, eat grass and then grow up to get ordered around by dogs. *DOGS*, LAMB.

ARGH! This picture almost turned me into the Hulk. My shirt actually ripped off. I also smashed my stapler, but that was unrelated. It also wasn't actually my stapler; I was borrowing it.

Stingrays forget that their name is a dead giveaway

Brad Thompson / Shutterstock Images LLC

I know you think you are going to get me to come over there and give you a big hug, Stingray. And, yeah, I am pretty impressed with your winning smile, I'm not going to lie. But you have 'sting' right there in your name. I mean, Manta Ray, no problem – let's hug like crazy. Devil Ray, okay, not really kosher, but I can handle that – bring it in. But Stingray? I'm gonna need something a lot more convincing than those soft eyes and flappy wings, buddy. Maybe, like, a signed agreement that you won't sting me.

Beyond that, Stingray, there isn't much I can do for you. So, please, stop smiling like that, or at least only get photographed from the top so no one can see it. It makes you look desperate.

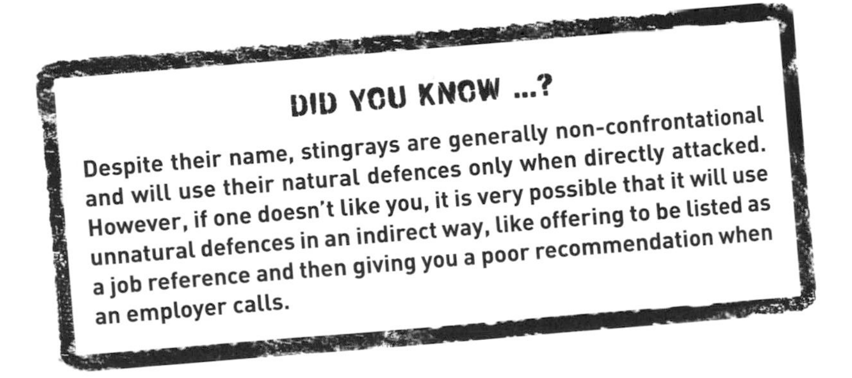

DID YOU KNOW ...?

Despite their name, stingrays are generally non-confrontational and will use their natural defences only when directly attacked. However, if one doesn't like you, it is very possible that it will use unnatural defences in an indirect way, like offering to be listed as a job reference and then giving you a poor recommendation when an employer calls.

One asshole (to scale)

Vicki Jedlicka, University of Nebraska–Lincoln Extension in Lancaster County

This egotistical little jerk was basically like 'Check me out, eh? EH?' and then when people didn't respond he was all 'Okay, maybe you don't understand, I AM ONLY ONE AND A HALF INCHES TALL' and stood next to a fucking ruler to illustrate his point.

Well, first of all, Quail, I AM THE ONLY ONE WHO IS ALLOWED TO USE CAPS LOCK IN THIS BOOK. And second, just because you are an impossibly small version of a bird doesn't make it okay to show it off. I know you grow up to be a bit of a dandy, so you have to go for it while you still got it, but you are going full-court press at the moment. I need you to slow down or face the consequences, you miniature bastard.

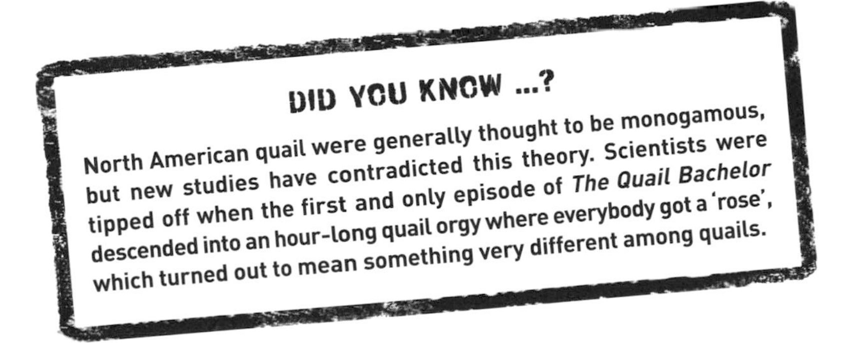
DID YOU KNOW ...?

North American quail were generally thought to be monogamous, but new studies have contradicted this theory. Scientists were tipped off when the first and only episode of *The Quail Bachelor* descended into an hour-long quail orgy where everybody got a 'rose', which turned out to mean something very different among quails.

I got your chi right here

Irena Kofman / Shutterstock Images LLC

Aw, poor Lemur. Busy day at work? Kids got you down? Concerned about the geopolitical turmoil in the Middle East? Yeah, meditation is probably a great idea. Why don't you just relax, turn off your 'thinking' brain and start using your 'feeling' brain.

Oh, wait. I just remembered you are a lemur. There is nothing stressful in your day except where to put your tail to make yourself look particularly cute. I realize now that your decision to take up meditation was just an excuse to show off your furry belly. STOP USING THE TRANSFORMATIVE POWER OF SELF-REFLECTION AGAINST ME. You may think your cunning daily routine has me won over, but I'm not even going to let it stress me out. At least I still have yoga.

Oh, shit, who taught this jackass yoga?

Luis César Tejo / Shutterstock Images LLC

I'm pretty sure bears don't need to be more supple, so I don't know what this guy is doing. I mean, we all know how elitist polar bears are, so it makes sense that they would want to throw in some yoga right before they grab a latte and head over to their Slow Food meeting. But I don't think this guy is even doing it right. You are supposed to get down LOW in the downward-facing bear position, idiot. And don't even pretend like you are just messing around, I know polar bears can't do anything half-assed. Whether it's having babies that bring new meaning to the word 'cute' or eating entire carcasses of seals, you sanctimonious little shits just have to be the best, don't you?

But really, what's with the stressed-out animals? It's not like humans have created an unsustainable march towards an Earth that is quickly becoming uninhabitable. YOU ASSHOLES HAVE IT EASY. Stop doing things created for humans to make them feel better about themselves, this is our time. You don't see me walking around a barren wasteland searching for food, do you?

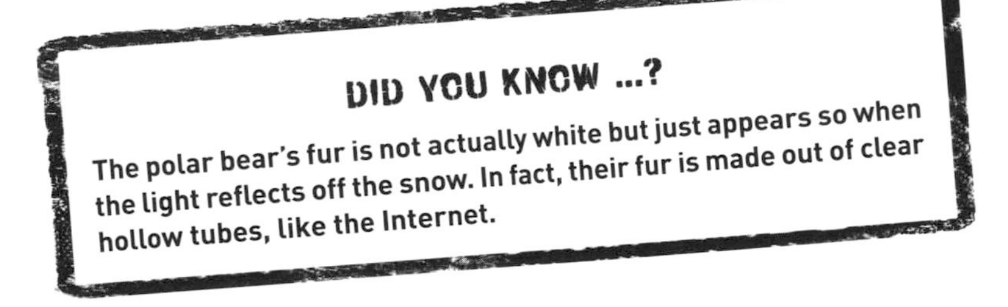

DID YOU KNOW ...?

The polar bear's fur is not actually white but just appears so when the light reflects off the snow. In fact, their fur is made out of clear hollow tubes, like the Internet.

I know you can hear me, Fox

Katherin Gaisser

Fox, let's be real with each other. I know you are pretending to sleep right now, because you can hear beetles walking on sand. So either you can turn those things off, or you are just playing around here. DO YOU THINK THIS IS FUNNY, FOX? DO YOU THINK THIS IS A GAME? You better not wake up right when I finish this page, Fox. I will not be happy.

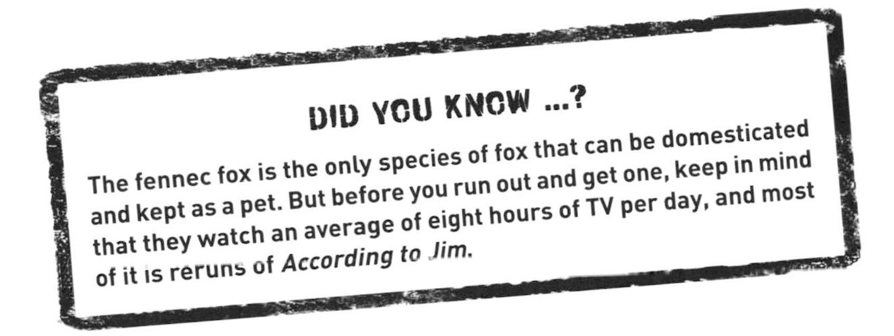

GODDAMMIT, FOX!

Katherin Gaisser

Don't believe this scumbag

Mausinda / Shutterstock Images LLC

I know this guy looks like he's been around for a while and he knows what he's talking about, but DO NOT TAKE FINANCIAL ADVICE FROM HIM. First of all, the viscacha is not a rabbit, it's a rodent, which takes him down a peg or two in terms of ability to really see what's going on from a broad perspective and think in terms of long-term solvency. Second, those whiskers come included with every member of the species, so he's really not as wise as he seems.

Quite frankly, Viscacha, I don't care how many times they let you on CNBC, you have no idea what you are talking about. I'm not going to 'take this opportunity during the downturn to invest in grass'. AND THANKS FOR THAT HOT TIP ON CIRCUIT CITY, MORON. THEY REALLY DID TURN IT AROUND, DIDN'T THEY? You'll be hearing from my attorney, Viscacha.

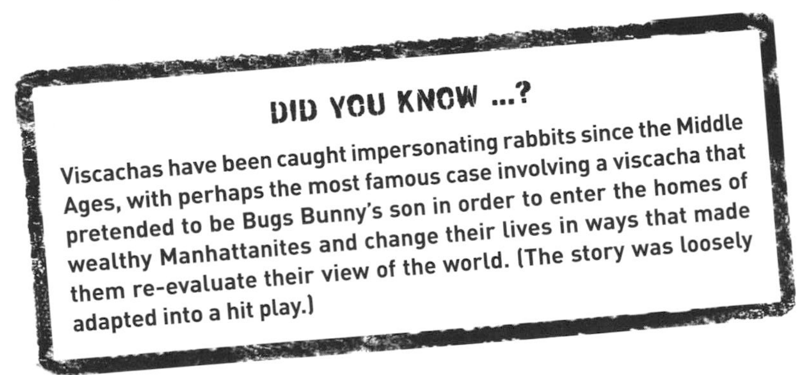

Baby flamingos make my job less fun

Eric Gevaert / Shutterstock Images LLC

Hey, Baby Flamingo, where did you get those giant-ass legs – THE OVERSIZED LEG DEPARTMENT?

Wait, hold on. This doesn't feel right. Sigh.

Baby Flamingo, your legs are really just too big. I mean, there's comically big, and then there's ridiculous. Here I am, trying to tell you off and make the world a better place, but those legs are so giant and you look so ridiculously helpless because of them that you are practically telling yourself off. And then what did you think? 'This isn't enough. I need to stand next to a grown-up flamingo, but only so that you can see its still comical but entirely acceptable long pink leg.' WHAT HAPPENED TO THE HAPPY MEDIUM, FLAMINGO? Well, I'm sick and tired of your extremes, Baby Flamingo, and I certainly won't be adding you as a co-author of my book, you spotlight-hogging asshole.

DID YOU KNOW ...?

No one knows why flamingos stand on one leg. However, most people believe that they do it just to annoy ornithologists, as flamingos are notoriously jealous of people with advanced degrees.

These assholes are taunting me

AP Photo

Hippo and Tortoise, this aggression will not stand. When you lie next to each other, and kiss each other, and lay your heads on each other, and do whatever else you sick fucks do that they can't include in children's books, it is like you are mugging me, but leaving my wallet and just taking my dignity. STOP BEING SUCH A STUDY IN CONTRASTS. I can tell you think this is funny, Hippo. You're looking at me like it is fucking hilarious. But, Tortoise, I am particularly disappointed in you. You are 130 years old; clearly you should know better by now. You've only got another fifty years to get your act together. These pictures are everywhere. Think of what your great-great-great-great-great-great-grandchildren will say to you when they see them. For shame, Tortoise.

DID YOU KNOW ...?

This hippo and tortoise friendship was formed in the aftermath of the 2004 tsunami in the Indian Ocean. This demonstrates that even out of something so tragic can come something so much worse in every way.

Squirrels that try to be productive members of society can suck it

Surinder Singh / www.surindersingh.org

You little fucker, you think you can just fucking waltz into our lives like nothing ever happened, but I know your kind, Squirrel. I turn my back for one second and you are causing power outages and breaking the noses of Finnish opera singers. So just go back to being hunched over nibbling on an acorn in my backyard, because you can stand there waiting for an invitation to my Christmas party all you want, but IT'S NOT GOING TO COME. You may have found my weakness for animals that stand on two legs, but I'm smarter than you, Squirrel. And I will defeat you.

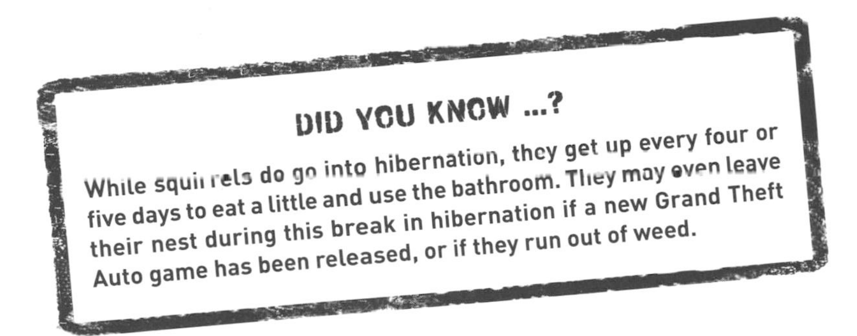

DID YOU KNOW ...?

While squirrels do go into hibernation, they get up every four or five days to eat a little and use the bathroom. They may even leave their nest during this break in hibernation if a new Grand Theft Auto game has been released, or if they run out of weed.

Monkey Overkill

Fame Pictures, Inc.

Monkey, I've got something to say, and it's about you biting that bar, and it's not going to be pretty.

You know, Monkey, if you had just sat there like a normal monkey, you would have been cute enough. Hell, you could have even fallen on your back and put all of your arms and legs up in the air, and I would have been fine with it. But biting that bar? Fuck you. Just. Fuck. You.

What conceited meerkats really want to do is direct

SouthWest News Service

Oh my God, you little highly social jerkoff. It's not enough that you get your OWN FUCKING SHOW, you have to be Ansel fucking Adams with the camera. But this is exactly what happens when animals get too popular, it all goes to their heads and they start to think they should be running the show. Guess what, Meerkat? NO ONE WANTS TO SEE YOUR POOR USE OF NEGATIVE SPACE. And, yeah, your exploration of morality in a post-9/11 society would be much more impactful if you weren't a fucking cannibal, you sicko.

Let's both you and me face it together, Meerkat. The only reason people pay attention to you is for your looks, and once those go, you will be replaced by a cuter, more talented animal. I'm thinking, oh, I don't know, ELEPHANT ESTATE. Terrified, aren't you, Meerkat? Get ready to find out who your friends really are.

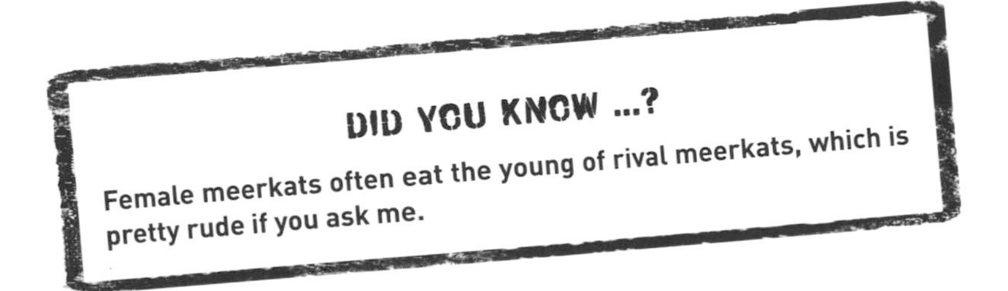

Petting zoo goats are like stuck-up celebrities with horns

photo by Derek White / www.scense.com

Petting zoos are a hotbed of animal hubris. With children constantly saying how cute they are, it's important to let the goats know that not everybody is on their dicks 24/7. This dandy here hasn't gotten nearly enough humble pie, because he apparently thinks he's next in line on the runway in fucking Milan. Ummm, not every goat gets to just lie around all day waiting for little six-year-olds to come and rub them behind the ears. Some goats actually have to work hard all day to find six-year-olds to rub them behind the ears.

What I'm trying to say, Goat, is that you can't have this carrot. I know I promised it to you earlier, in a moment of weakness, but I also know goats can't use tape recorders, and there are limited legal avenues that you can pursue. TIME TO FEND FOR YOURSELF, GOATS. Hey—

NO-

photo by Derek White / www.scense.com

Where did you get that?!

Ah ... dammit.

Um, I can see you

Matt Greenwood

Cow, what the hell do you think you are doing hiding behind that tree? You do realize you are a cow, right? It's not likely that you are going to be able to keep a low profile, seeing as cows are so large that they are a metaphor for fat people. I (almost) respect the effort, but I don't care that your horns kind of match the tree, that emo haircut of yours is not botanical.

And what kind of cow has horns anyway? You are supposed to be black and white, and I'm supposed to drive by you in my car on road trips and lean out the window and say 'Moo'. Get back to work being harmless and lying in the grass. STOP RUINING MY VACATIONS BY WANTING MORE OUT OF LIFE, COW.

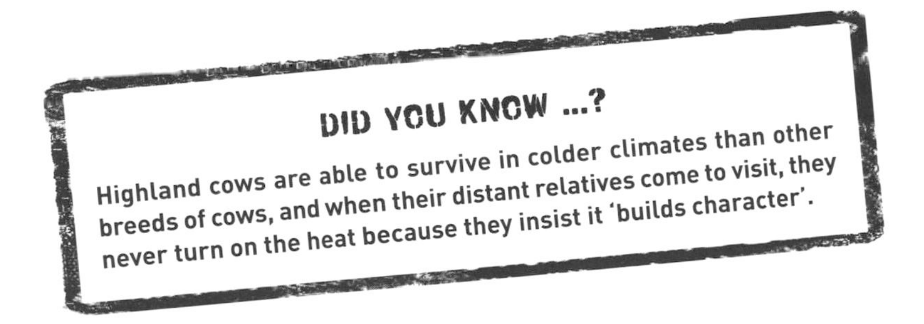

Oh, now orange isn't cute enough?

Scott Dart / iStockphoto LP

What the hell do you think you are doing, Tiger? You are destroying my ability to function as a responsible member of society, what with your extremely rare and yet equally extremely cute appearance. At this point in life you have two choices: grow the fuck up and dye your hair orange like a NORMAL FUCKING TIGER or just jam a knife into my skull and put an end to my misery. Dammit, Tiger. I literally hate you.

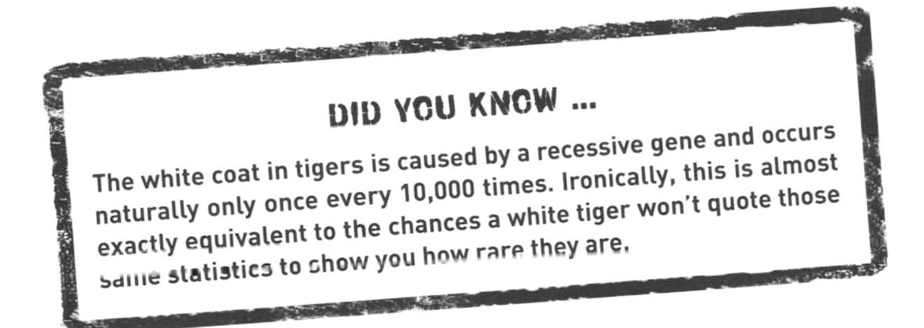

Someone get this fat fuck a carrot

© Jerry Weinstein / www.naturegraphics.net

Hey, Prairie Dog, I didn't realize doughnuts were native to the grasslands of North America! You're so fat, you make a capybara look like an African pygmy mouse!

Seriously, though, Prairie Dog. You are really fat. This makes it very difficult for me, because the fact that your feet aren't touching the ground and your arms are kind of hanging down on your fat folds is fucking cute as shit. Am I supposed to feel bad for you? Is this what you wanted, Prairie Dog? Damn you and your scheming ways.

DID YOU KNOW ...?

Prairie dogs kiss other members of their group when they greet them, which can be cute until they've been drinking and start slipping each other some tongue.

Resorting to props is fucking pathetic

© Gerard Fritz / AccentAlaska.com

Raccoons don't have to try. So what does this asshole think he is doing? Is it so hard to just stand on your hind legs or hug your tail? YOU LOOK LIKE A FUCKING ROBBER FOR CHRIST'S SAKE. So I don't presume to understand just what you might have gone through in your life to get to the point where you have to do this, Raccoon, but you better get out from behind that fucking tree right now. Or I am NEVER throwing out my trash again.

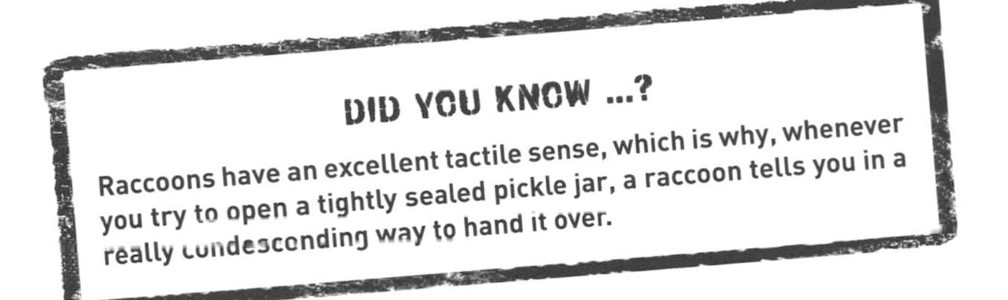

DID YOU KNOW ...?

Raccoons have an excellent tactile sense, which is why, whenever you try to open a tightly sealed pickle jar, a raccoon tells you in a really condescending way to hand it over.

Cliché Capybaras

© Kevinschafer.com

Am I wrong, or did someone just take one capybara and Photoshop it in different sizes and positions into the same picture? GET A NEW LOOK, CAPYBARA. At this point, I'm pretty sure that meeting one capybara means you have met them all. But in the end, who wants to meet a capybara anyway? They are giant rats that think just because they have webbed feet and let you pet them that they can roam the earth for millions of years and no one will ever call them on their shit. Well, you know what, Capybara? Maybe you would actually deserve my affection if you started showing just a little bit of interest in my life. But instead you just stand there with that smug look on your face, time and time again. Not very original, Capybara. How long do you really think you can ride this wave before I stop feeding you this cantaloupe?

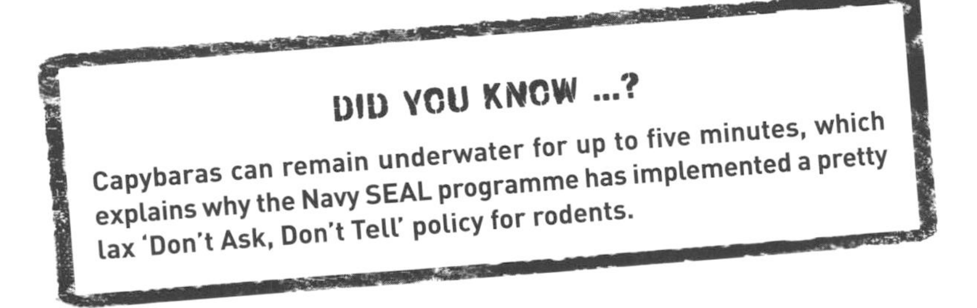

This bear is essentially raping my soul

Huetter, C. / Arco Digital Images

So basically this totally thoughtless motherfucker decided regular bears weren't cute enough. His solution? GIVE HIMSELF NATURAL FUCKING EYEGLASSES. Then, becoming the single cutest animal on the face of the earth, he lay on his fucking back so we could all see his goddamn belly, and then furtively glanced in our direction, thereby rendering any potential defence against his advances totally useless. Well played, Bear. I'm going to go take a shower now.

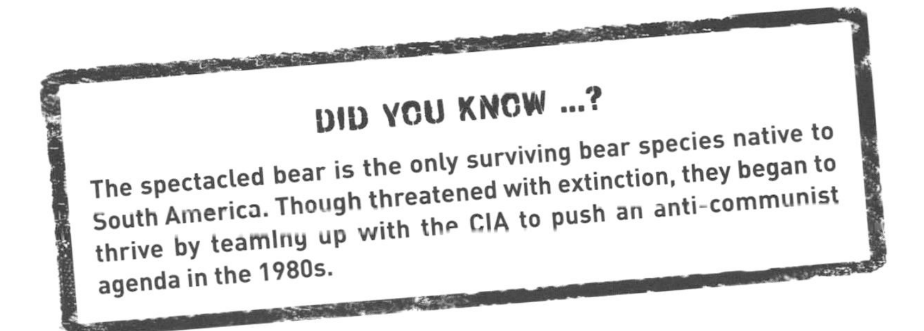

Egotistical deer always think they are making your day

Howard Sandler / Shutterstock Images LLC

Deer like to take time out of their busy days roaming the forest and eating leaves to come into a clearing so onlookers can get a glimpse of them. They always claim to do this 'for the people', but it's really because deer are huge attention whores. If they walked out into the open and no one turned to look, they would probably do something embarrassing like run in front of a car and just stand there, practically begging for someone to notice them.

Well, today is the day, Deer, because I am NOT impressed. I'm just having breakfast on my porch here; I didn't come outside to be awed by the planet's beauty and the fleeting nature of our time on Earth. So why don't you wipe that smirk off your face, the one that's like you're saying, 'This is really gonna make their day', and back right up into that forest and go find me something interesting to look at, like one of those 3-D posters.

DID YOU KNOW ...?

Deer raise their tails to warn other deer of danger in the area. Considering how many deer had a clear view of the situation, this means a lot of them wanted Bambi's mother dead.

You better be in imminent danger, Monkey

© CNImaging/Photoshot

Monkey, I swear to God, if there isn't a gun just off camera or a man with a giant hammer running towards you, you are in SERIOUS FUCKING TROUBLE. I understand that in the event of an emergency you are advised to grab anything else in the area that is cute and therefore double your cute defences, but, Monkey, THIS IS DEFCON 2-LEVEL SHIT. Come to think of it, if everyone had a monkey just out of reach of a dove, perhaps we could bring about world peace. Fuck you, Monkey, for hoarding the technology.

Porcupine fish send out mixed messages

Raymond Connetta / Shutterstock Images LLC

Good lord, you smiling asshole. What is going on with the fish lips and big eyes? YOU ARE SO FUCKING CUTE I WANT TO HUG YOU AND NAME YOU GARY. But I know better, Porcupine Fish. You may me be smiling and having a great time now in your little undersea neon world, but next thing I know I'll come too close and you'll

Push me away

© Jeffrey Jeffords / Divegallery.com

The truth is, Porcupine Fish, I don't know if you could ever really get close to anyone. Before you love someone, you have to love yourself, and I'm worried about the time you're putting in. You drift from place to place with no purpose in life, and you couldn't even expend enough effort to give yourself a name, you just picked something with spines and added 'fish' to the name. You may get a lot of attention now, but sooner or later everyone is going to grow tired of your shenanigans, and you will realize what a shallow, empty life you lead. I'm not going to be there to pick up the pieces, Porcupine Fish. You can go to hell for all I care.

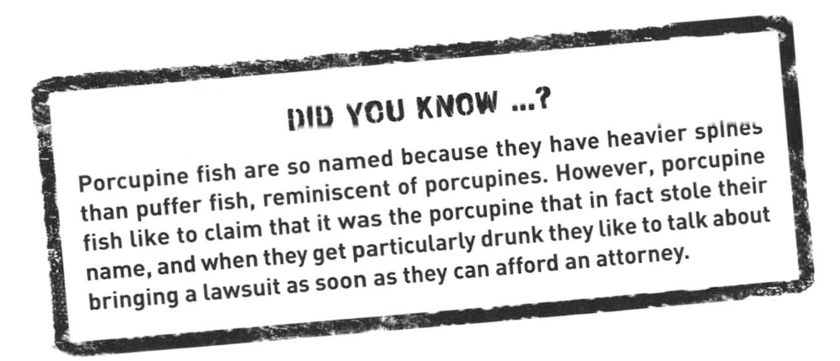

DID YOU KNOW ...?

Porcupine fish are so named because they have heavier spines than puffer fish, reminiscent of porcupines. However, porcupine fish like to claim that it was the porcupine that in fact stole their name, and when they get particularly drunk they like to talk about bringing a lawsuit as soon as they can afford an attorney.

Sea horses make me less interested in real horses

RbbrDckyBK / iStockphoto LP

FUCK! Horses were all prancey and I could ride them and shit. It was totally kickass. At one point, I even said, 'Who needs the ocean when you have horses?' And I lived my life like that meant something. Now I see a sea horse and that all goes out the window. How did you get the head of a horse? That shit is I-N-S-A-N-E.

Oftentimes, animals with combo names are total crap, like that porcupine fish from the last page. (wtf? Still not over it? Get a real name, loser.) But this fucker really lives up to his billing, and I'm not going to let him get away with it. Yeah, I see the curved tail, and I know the males have babies (apparently nature's rules don't apply to everyone if you're 'special' enough). But that doesn't give him the right to simultaneously look like a horse, some coral, a fluke and a Creamsicle. Pick a style and run with it, Sea Horse. Stop freaking me out, and let me have the normal horses that eat apples and let flies sit on their eyeballs.

Sneaky hedgehogs want it both ways

© Sean Sosik-Hamor / HamorHollow.com

Just because you have your mouth opened like that doesn't mean I can't see those giant needles on your entire body ready to impale me, Hedgehog. You think I'm afraid, but I also don't want to hurt you because you're too cute, right? Well, you know what, Hedgehog? You cross me, in ANY way, and I WILL NOT HESITATE TO DESTROY YOU. Believe that, Hedgehog. Now watch your fucking step.

DID YOU KNOW ...?

Male hedgehogs can have as many as 500 spines on their back, but will often claim to have as many as 750 just to seem tougher than they actually are.

Seals are always looking for a handout

Lightphase Photography / Shutterstock Images LLC

This seal can obviously see I am eating a Starburst at the moment (apple-flavoured) and expects me to give him some. Honestly, I think this seal must be stupid, because there is no fucking way I am going to give my Starburst, which I work hard every day to pay for, to a GODDAMNED, GOOD-FOR-NOTHING SEAL just because he looks at me with giant droopy eyes when I know damn well all he does all day is lounge around on rocks, getting fat. Besides, A, I already finished the Starburst, and, B, he didn't give me any kind of home address where I could send it even if I still had some. So go eat a fish or something, Seal. Stop expecting everyone else to pick up your slack.

Great, now I have to live in a pigsty

IA98 / Shutterstock Images LLC

What the hell, Pig? MOST INCONVENIENT TIMING EVER. I have on these nice trousers, just walking by the sty, and you have to come over here and push your nose in my face. Real nice, Pig, real fucking nice. I bet you think you are so great, just trotting over here to show me your big ears and your sloppy face. Does it amuse you to throw my life into disarray with your tempting glances?

So, yeah, I'm coming, but I'm not happy about it. Just give me a second to call my boss and quit my job before I climb over this fence and start the first day of the rest of my life, you manipulative asshole.

What a blue-footed sleaze

Mariko Yuki / Shutterstock Images LLC

First I thought this blue-footed booby was just doing a cute little dance, which is bad enough (personally, I can dance fucking circles around this loser). But it turns out this is a fucking mating ritual, which basically means dude is hitting on me.

I'm not really sure what makes you think I'm interested, Booby, other than the fact that I took an eight-hour plane ride and a four-hour boat ride, and went on an hour-and-a-half hike to see your unique display of evolutionary courtship in action. I'm still not going to run off with a sexed-up wanker like you. Anyway, I'm pretty sure your lady friend flew off to find some other-coloured feet. Blue kind of says last year, asshole. Get with the times.

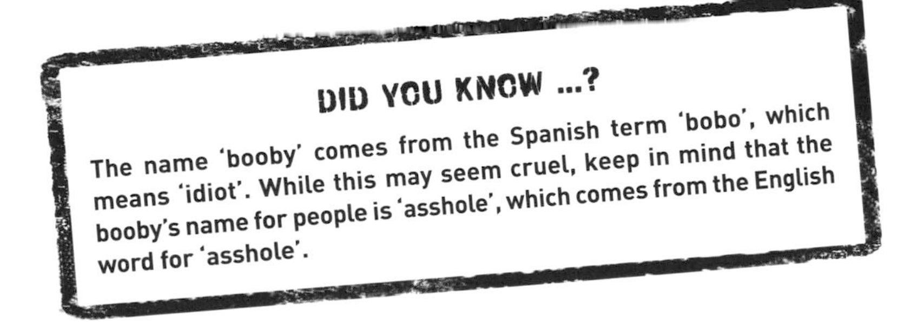

DID YOU KNOW ...?

The name 'booby' comes from the Spanish term 'bobo', which means 'idiot'. While this may seem cruel, keep in mind that the booby's name for people is 'asshole', which comes from the English word for 'asshole'.

Rare animals can be a real drag

Zoological Society of London

Thanks a lot, Zoological Society of London. Yesterday, I had no idea the long-eared jerboa existed. Today, he's hopping around all over like he owns the fucking joint. Well, here's a little bit of info now that you are on the big stage, Long-Eared Jerboa: I don't need you, the people don't need you, and you sure as hell aren't going to get special treatment from me just because you are a combination of a mouse and a kangaroo with a little bit of giant ears thrown in just to be fucking difficult. And why are all the pictures of you at night? WHAT ARE YOU HIDING, JERBOA? Whatever. I was living my life long before I knew what you were, Long-Eared Jerboa, and I will go on living my life long after I have set you as my desktop picture.

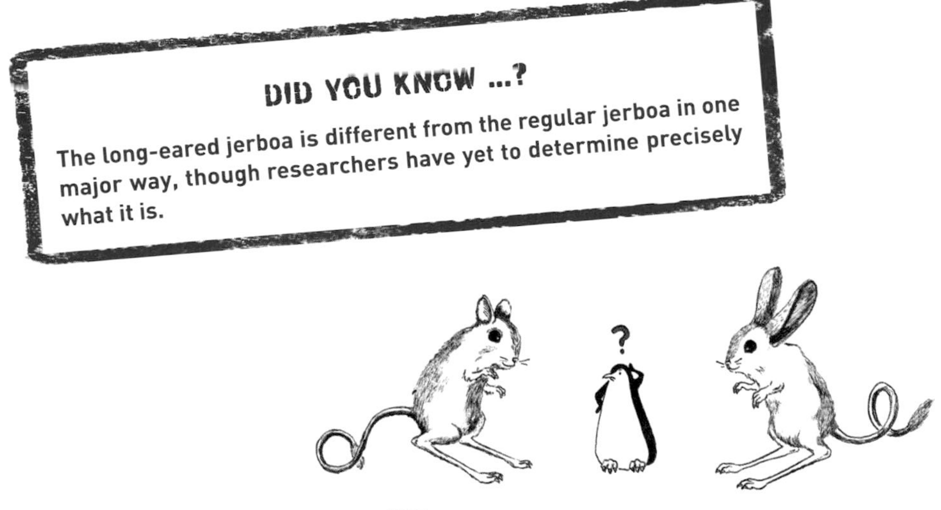

Swans are nature's Porsche drivers

Adrian Pingstone

You know, there was once an ugly duckling who got picked on all of the time by the other ducks, who couldn't understand why the duckling was so ugly. But then it turned out that the duckling wasn't really a duck at all, but was in fact a TOTAL FUCKING DICK.

Take this world-class wanker, for example. Everyone is just hanging out, having a good time, and Mr. 'My Wingspan is Bigger than Yours' decides to unload on the scene. Even his swan friend is embarrassed. He probably does it all the fucking time, because, let's be honest, that's just what swans do. Me personally, I wouldn't be caught dead with a fucking swan.

Unsatisfied wombats don't know how good they have it

Thanks to: Sydney Wildlife World

You know, Wombat, all I do is love you. But is that good enough for you? No, you have to look at wombats in magazines and ask, 'Why can't I look like that?' Well, I'm not here to boost your ego; I'm here to have a life with you. SO STOP FISHING FOR COMPLIMENTS, WOMBAT. I'm tired of you pretending like you're not standing there with your cute little fat nose and pudgy legs. And what would I want with a fucking attention whore like they have in those magazines anyway? Sure, I was looking, anyone would look. But seriously, Wombat, you're making a scene. You know what? Don't call me anymore.

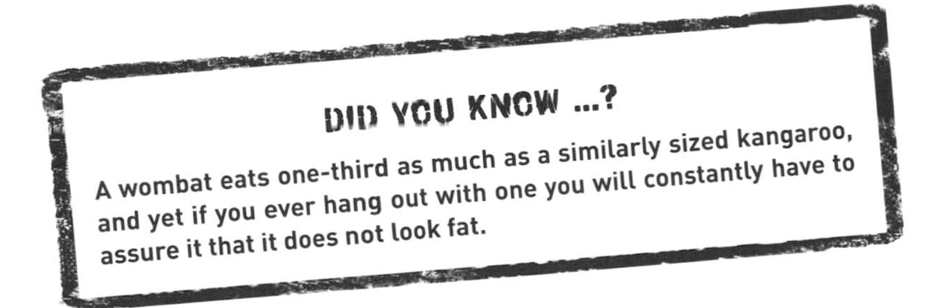

Lions even bore themselves

Camilo Torres / Shutterstock Images LLC

I'm not really sure where this 'King of the Jungle' designation came from, but, honestly, that is the biggest load of horseshit ever. Look at this dude – he looks like he's ready to put on a pair of slippers and turn in for the night. I seriously wonder if the lion hasn't been resting on its laurels for the past few hundred years, and no one has actually tested one of these things. Like, some lion started a whisper campaign about how he was a real badass, and because the mane makes him look bigger than he actually is, no one wanted to fuck with him. WELL, GUESS WHAT, LION, TODAY IS YOUR UNLUCKY DAY.

I'm sorry, what?

Four Oaks / Shutterstock Images LLC. Below: Stefan Petru Andronache / Shutterstock Images LLC

Oh, no, I was talking
to this guy

Not you – we're buddies, right? Can I get you anything? No? Okay, well, you let me know.

DID YOU KNOW ...?

An adult male lion requires an average of fifteen pounds of meat per day, but never brings any food for himself when he is invited to dinner parties.

Why are you doing this to me?

Shutterstock Images LLC

Yes. Okay? Yes. I want to come sit on the hammock. Are you happy? This whole situation is just awful, ever since I found this photo I've been a complete mess. I've started calling up people in the neighbourhood who have hammocks and asking them if they've had any bear visits lately. I hired the CIA to evaluate the photo and figure out what type of trees are in the background so I can figure out what is the most likely location of the hammock. Do you have any idea how much time it takes to re-create a photo in a three-dimensional holographic workspace?

Jesus Christ, Bear, not only are you forcing me into this situation, you are making me come up with cutesy fucking headlines like 'I thought you said you were going to mow the lawn' and 'Sleepy the Bear says only you can prevent afternoon napping'. I HAVE A REPUTATION TO UPHOLD, BEAR. Get off the hammock and go eat something with blood in it so I can think about the dichotomy between your cuteness and your insatiable thirst for flesh.

DID YOU KNOW ...?

If you live in an area where there have been bear sightings, it is important to keep your trash sealed and not leave food out. This is not just because the bear will become too familiar with the area and have to be forcibly removed, but because if the bear does not like what you have to offer, he will write a scathing opinion piece in the local paper the next day.

Start fucking, Donkey

ANIMALS ANIMALS © Sunset/Proust, Frederic

AHHHHHHGH. There is a long-haired donkey, and it's named the Baudet de Poitou? Ho. Lee. Shit. How can there only be 400 of you cute little fuckers!?! This is a serious problem, seeing as I personally need 400 of you. You better find a mate and start knocking boots, Donkey, so you can sprout up like American Apparels. I don't understand how you can be such prudes, seeing as you are French. What, are you saving yourself for the right donkey? YOU AREN'T WEARING A FUCKING PROMISE RING, ARE YOU, DONKEY? BECAUSE I AM GOING TO BE SERIOUSLY UPSET. Anyway, stop being so picky, you're a donkey. This is serious business. Make it happen.

DID YOU KNOW ...?

There were only forty-four Baudet de Poitou in the world in the 1970s. Then, in 1982, Marvin Gaye released 'Sexual Healing'.

The scourge of strange-looking animals must end!

EcoPrint / Shutterstock Images LLC

You know what, Giraffe? You think just because you kind of look like a horse, but have a giant neck and these two weird things between your ears that I have no idea what they are, that you can just get away with coming up to my second-storey window and eating my toast. But you are WRONG, Giraffe. DEAD FUCKING WRONG.

Okay, maybe you can have my toast. But don't you FUCKING DARE touch my banana, Giraffe. You've been warned.

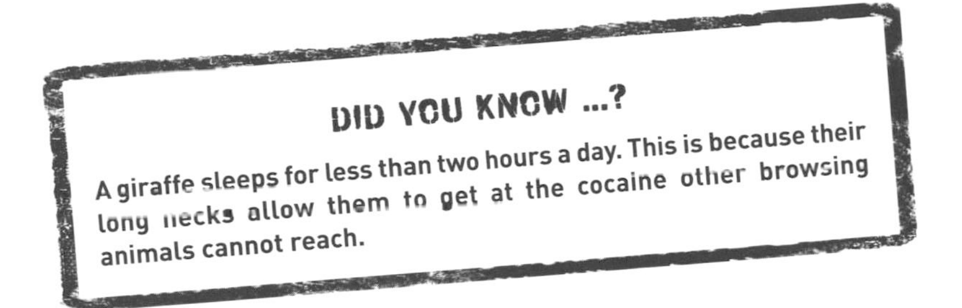

DID YOU KNOW ...?

A giraffe sleeps for less than two hours a day. This is because their long necks allow them to get at the cocaine other browsing animals cannot reach.

Dolphin swagger makes me sick

L.S. Luecke / Shutterstock Images LLC

Oh my god, Dolphin, you smug little shit. What is with that smile? You think just because you can recognize yourself in a mirror you can go around acting like your shit doesn't smell? (It smells, right?) You need to wipe that smile off your face, Dolphin, or I'm going to come in there, have a religious-like experience swimming with you, and then wipe it off for you.

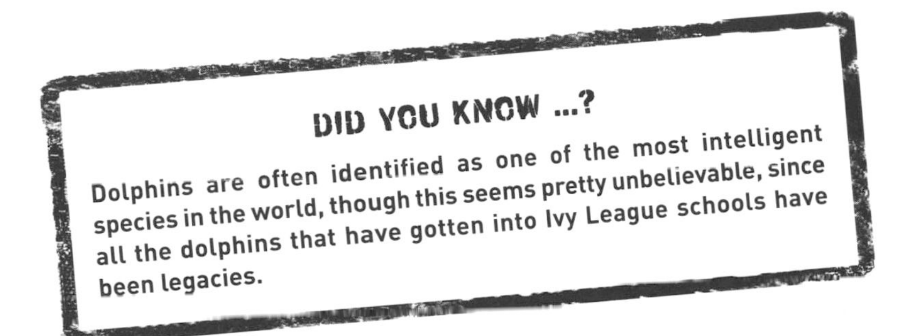

The Tibetan fox thinks he's better than you

© Milo Burcham

I just want you people to drink in this world-class wanker known as the Tibetan fox. Have you ever seen such a holier-than-thou fucking look on a non-dolphin before? I'm not one for slapping foxes, as I generally think they know what they've done, but this one really has that look, like the asshole boyfriend of the girl the main guy wants in an '80s movie. Unsurprisingly, he is extremely rare. That's probably because he thinks if he has too many babies, some of them will turn out to be commoners and he wouldn't be able to show his square face at the country club anymore.

How's your ivory tower, Tibetan Fox? I'm sure it must be terribly stressful to stand in judgment of the rest of us little people, so why don't you just retire to your cabin and play lacrosse? You know what, on second thought, WHY DON'T YOU WANDER THE DESERT LOOKING FOR RODENTS? Some of us have to work for a living, Tibetan Fox. We don't get everything handed to us by a lifetime of hunting and scavenging, you stuckup snob.

DID YOU KNOW ...?

Tibetan foxes mostly eat rodents, although they refuse to eat anything but organic, free-range rodents that come from within one hundred miles of their farmer's market.

Tortoises always want someone else to do their dirty work

Caroline Tolsma / Shutterstock Images LLC

Are you kidding me, Tortoise? You are so lazy you can't get up and go see what's going on over there? You don't think someone else is going to take pity on you and just tell you what it is, do you? Because it sure as shit isn't going to be this guy. And you know, Tortoise, just because you are like 3,000 years old doesn't mean you shouldn't use some lotion once in a while. That neck looks like a petrified tree trunk, and not in a good way. MOISTURIZE, TORTOISE.

DID YOU KNOW ...?

The oldest living thing ever was actually not a tortoise, as many people believe, but a koi fish that lived to be more than 200 years old. The fish eventually succumbed to jealous-tortoise-related injuries.

Iguanas are living in the past

Lori Martin / Shutterstock Images LLC

Not to be a dick or anything, Iguana, but you're not a fucking dinosaur. I know you roam around showing off your scaly skin, your beady little eyes and your nose holes. And, yes, I've seen your tongue. But let me ask you a few questions. Can I ride you? Do you have answering machine messages from Steven Spielberg? WERE YOU ON MY SHOES WHEN I WAS EIGHT???

So don't waddle or slither or whatever you do over here and pretend that you rule the Earth. WELCOME TO THE QUATERNARY PERIOD, IGUANA.

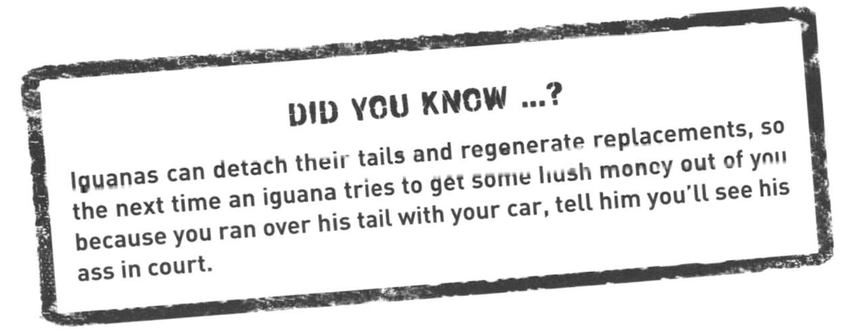

DID YOU KNOW ...?

Iguanas can detach their tails and regenerate replacements, so the next time an iguana tries to get some hush money out of you because you ran over his tail with your car, tell him you'll see his ass in court.

Thanks for 'gracing' us with your presence

Lazareva Evgeniya / iStockphoto LP

I get it, Whale, you're busy. I've only been on this FUCKING BOAT for three and a half hours waiting for you, and the only thing I've seen so far is my lunch from earlier. It's not like you spend your entire goddamn life in the ocean, so I see why you would only come up for basically a split second. Personally, if someone was going to all this trouble specifically to see me, I would take time out of my BUSY-ASS SCHEDULE to at least stop by the boat and make some small talk, maybe have some salmon. But I understand, Whale: places to go, 500 pounds of food to eat. I'll be fine. The real question here, Whale, is will you be fine? Can you really live with yourself? Maybe you need to make a change.

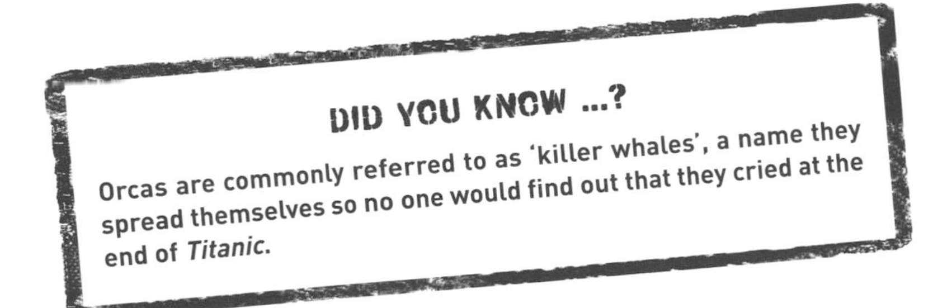

Coatis fight dirty

A.J. Maher

Damn you, Coati, you think that just by coming over and putting your stubby little legs and long nose against that foot you can single-handedly bring down the entire person attached to it. WELL, IT'S NOT GOING TO WORK, OSAMA BIN COATI. I don't know what kind of sick fantasies of being a hero get into your head, but freedom from your fuzzy belly and cute little tail will prevail.

As a people, we must band together against this until-now unknown threat. I don't know how we allowed an animal to get this cute and this bold, but we must stop it now. Just remember, it is important to maintain our composure and not fall victim to such reckless temptations as purchasing coffee mugs with coatis on them and writing love songs in their honour like 'I Would Do Anything for Coatis (Including That)' or 'My Heart Will Go On (Because of Coatis)'. If we do that, the coatis will already have won.

DID YOU KNOW ...?

Male coatis live alone except during the brief mating season, making coatis the personal heroes of married men throughout the world. Of course, that means coati societies are run entirely by women, and men only show up once every year to continue the species, so really it's a win–win.

What is this otter trying to prove?

David Gomez / iStockphoto LP

I'm on to you, Otter. You can't speak, so why are you putting your flippers up to your mouth as if you want to focus your screaming on someone far away? ANSWER THE QUESTION, OTTER! And I know you aren't trying to do a remake of *Home Alone*, because otters don't watch movies, they just read the newspaper. There's only one explanation here. You want my heart to melt into a puddle of water. Well, it's not going to work, Otter. So you can go to hell.

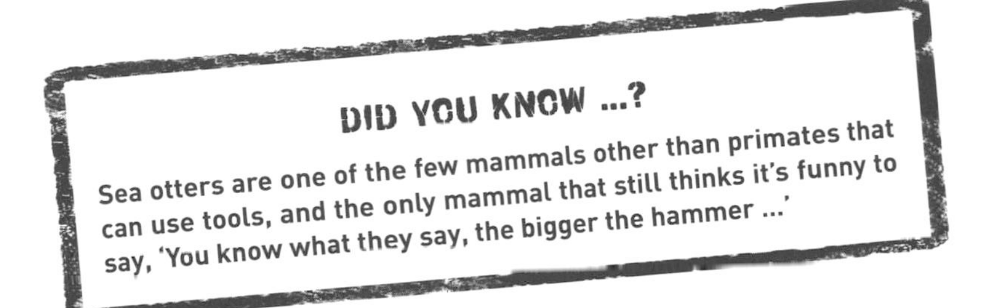

DID YOU KNOW ...?

Sea otters are one of the few mammals other than primates that can use tools, and the only mammal that still thinks it's funny to say, 'You know what they say, the bigger the hammer ...'

This bunny wants to ambush your sensibilities

Photographer TK / Shutterstock Images LLC

A teaching moment from *Fk You, Penguin.***

Bunny, what the hell do you think you are doing? Those people out there are just trying to have a nice walk in the woods, and here you are, waiting for the perfect moment to pounce on them and tear their insides out, hop by excruciating hop. STOP TRYING TO CAUSE A SPONTANEOUSLY CUTE INCIDENT. Did you think I wouldn't see you? Did you think you could just go around hiding in the dark corners of the world, working to undermine everything that holds civilized society together? You disgust me, Bunny.

LESSON: Never walk through a garden or a jungle without being aware of the distinct possibility that there could be some ridiculously cute asshole bunny crouched in the shadows, ready to pounce and violate your sacred sense of decency.

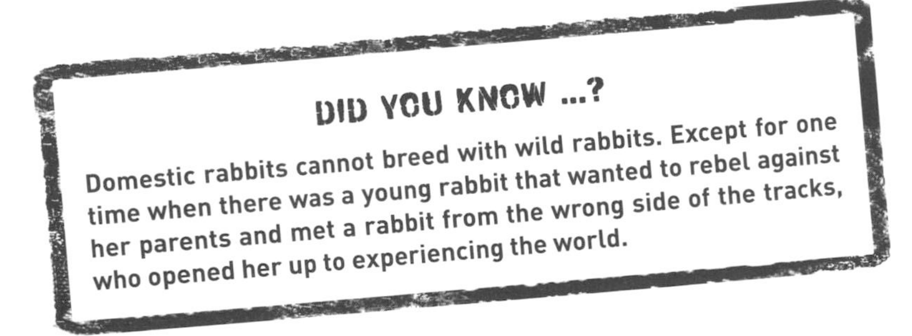

Llamas will break your heart without so much as a 'My bad'

Robert Pernell / Shutterstock Images LLC

So here I am looking at pictures of llamas online, because who doesn't love llamas, right? (Penguins, those jealous fucks.) And what do I come across but an article about this older llama that died in 2006, making the zoo where it lived very sad. The llama's name was Chief, and it had a severe colic reaction, WHICH TOTALLY FUCKING RUINED MY SUNDAY.

At least move back to Peru or something, so we can imagine you frolicking forever. Funny-looking mouths come with a responsibility to not play with our emotions.

Badger bravado doesn't fool anyone

John Pitcher / iStockphoto LP

Dude, put the hair down. I realize I'm getting 'dangerously' close to your burrow, but I have some news for you: you aren't intimidating anyone. In fact, the only thing I'm thinking right now is how I want to take you home and have a daughter for the sole purpose of letting her dress you up in pretty outfits so I can take pictures of you and upload them to the Internet. Next time you want to scare someone, make sure you don't have adorable facial markings and a furry belly.

This is not to say you should prance around like you are untouchable. Let me tell you, Badger, you're no penguin. Shit, you aren't even a meerkat. So don't get a big head and think you can melt my heart, Badger, because IT'S GOING TO TAKE A LOT MORE THAN JUST A FURRY BELLY TO WIN THIS GUY OVER. So calm down, take a deep breath and try again without so much fucking attitude.

ANIMALS ANIMALS © Dalton, Stephen

Honestly, Axolotl, if you don't stop existing right now, I'm going to tear my eyes out and then eat them, in the hope that this would somehow be so traumatic that I would never have to think about you ever again. You might finally put the whole intelligent design argument to rest. (Does anyone really want to think about God doing acid?) On the other hand, I can't possibly think of an evolutionary reason for you to look so ridiculous, you amphibious motherfucker. Are you trying to blend into a Keith Haring painting?

Just because you have a weird-looking smiley face where a normal face should be doesn't mean I'm gonna ignore the fact that you can't even metamorphosize your crazy ass. EPIC EVOLUTIONARY FAIL, AXOLOTL. Maybe you should think a little less about creeping people the fuck out and a little more about stimulating your thyroid. You probably make the best argument ever to stay out of the water. I'll take my quarter of the earth's surface, Axolotl; now leave me the fuck alone.

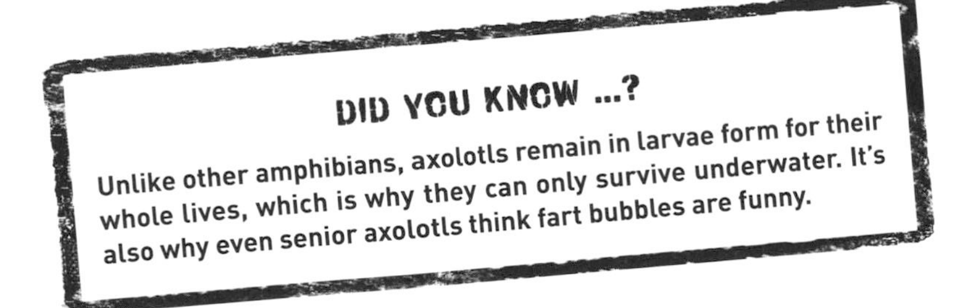

Elephants never forget to be total show-offs

Todd Hackwelder / Shutterstock Images LLC

What's that, Elephant? You have a large trunk? I had no idea, because it's not like you are putting it DIRECTLY IN FRONT OF MY FUCKING FACE. You know, I'm pretty tall, too. I can reach the top shelf in my kitchen. I also spray water out of my nose to bathe myself practically every day. So, please, stop pretending that just because you can do maths and recognize your buddies you should get a fucking Presidential Medal of Honour. Hey, there's Jim, with four other friends whom I recognize, which makes five people total. NOT THAT HARD ELEPHANT, STEP YOUR GAME UP.

Is it just me, or are baby animals really being dicks lately?

EcoPrint / Shutterstock Images LLC

I had a thought last night, Baby Elephant, and it involved you pulling out all the stops to get me on your side. That thought was that I hate you, Baby Elephant. All you do is stand in your African Shangri-la with your trunk and your ears and your little baby elephant smile, and I'm just supposed to sit here in my crumbling empire and take it. It seems like you aren't alone, either, as baby animals everywhere are really taking a turn for the worse. Well guess what, Baby Elephant, I'm not going to let you use the fact that you are a minor as an excuse for your shitty behaviour. I know you think you're a star but put the fucking ears away, YOU AREN'T DUMBO, BABY ELEPHANT. If you are going to act like a hardened criminal, it's time you learn the cold hard truths of the world.

And yeah, I know you thought you could get away with it because I just told off an elephant on the last page, but fuck you, they're my rules and I can break them whenever I want.

Secretly fucked-up animals always ruin my day

JJ Morales / Shutterstock Images LLC

Oh, man, what is this thing? A binturong? THAT NAME IS HILARIOUS!!! Wait, wait, it's also called a bearcat? I love bears, AND I love cats! Oh, wow, you're sleeping ... Who's a cute little bearcat? You are, that's who, yes you adora—

Arthur Ng Heng Kui / Shutterstock Images LLC

What. The. Fuck. Binturong? What's up? I was trying to have a good time. Why do you have to scare the shit out of me? You need to calm down, Binturong, rethink what's going on here. Just 'cause you have a bushy tail and are named after two all-time animals doesn't mean you can sleep like a cute little bastard and have babies named fucking bintlets (BINTLETS, I TELL YOU) and no one will care that you are a fucking psychopath. There are two sides of the animal world, Binturong. You need to pick one.

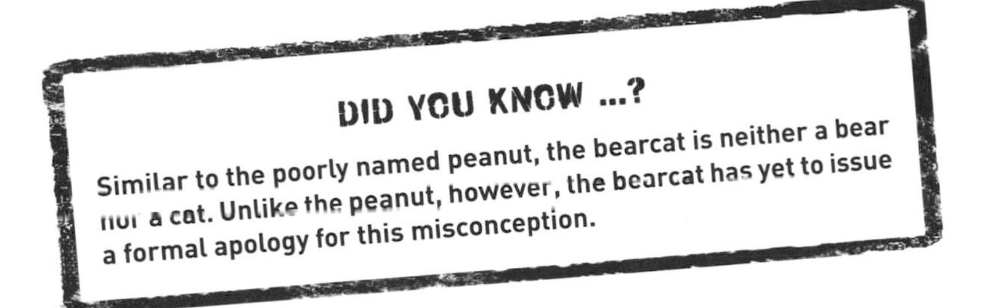

Snow leopards: rare, majestic, dickish

Vassil

Oh, no, don't turn around, Snow Leopard. I'll just talk to your giant-ass tail. What's the deal with that thing, anyway? Do you lift weights with it? What exactly do you need a tail the size of a large boa constrictor for? Are you cleaning out chimneys?

Nothing, huh? Okay, Snow Leopard. I see what's going on here. You're too busy being an obscure cat. But you know, Snow Leopard, I have feelings, too. Sure, I may not have a tail, and there are more than six billion of me, so I'm not 'SUPER FUCKING SPECIAL GUY' like you. But I'm on to you, Snow Leopard. I think it would be a good idea for you to keep your eyes open, because your tail and I are starting to develop a very special bond, and pretty soon you could be on the way out around here. Start showing us both some more attention, and maybe – MAYBE – we can all work something out.

Red panda trying to steal panda thunder

Thorsten Rust / Shutterstock Images LLC

Ummm ... excuse me? Red Panda? WHO DO YOU THINK YOU ARE TRYING TO FOOL? Pandas do things like serve me bad Chinese food in mall food courts, you little sneaky jerk-off. When was the last time your pregnancy was featured on the six o'clock news? And just because you are holding bamboo doesn't make you a panda, BELIEVE ME, I'VE TRIED. You are a fox or a raccoon, or some kind of rodent or something.

And why are you making yourself look taller than you actually are? No one is fooled by your reach for higher bamboo; there's plenty of good bamboo at red panda level. Or are you just trying to look powerful and dignified so I'll take you home and start a breeding programme? Are you that desperate to prevent your species from total annihilation? AND STOP TAKING UP SO MUCH MEMORY WHEN I OPEN MULTIPLE TABS.

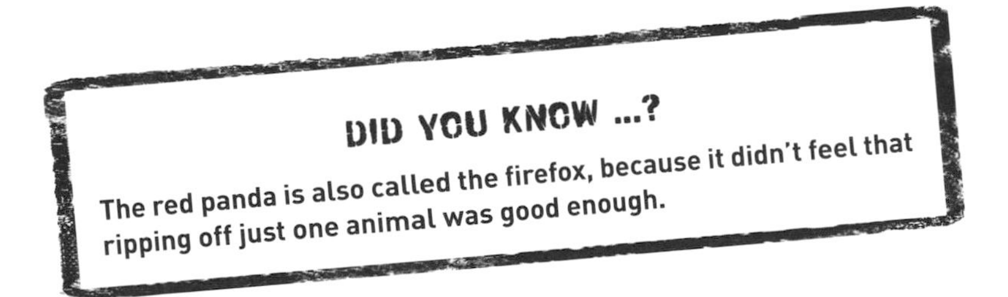

South Korea is the real Korean threat to humanity

Photo by RNL Bio Co. Ltd. via Getty Images

What the hell, South Korea? You guys seem so awesome, what with your delicious food, nice electronics and Internet addictions. You are like Japan but without the creepy porn (I mean this in a good way). So what are you trying to pull by cloning puppies? Are you seriously telling me one of those puppies isn't cute enough, YOU NEED THE SAME FUCKING PUPPY TWICE?!?! A normal country (like, say, Peru) wouldn't even need the whole puppy, it would be cool with just that impossibly pink nose.

I used to think you were the 'cool' Korea. People would badmouth Korea, and I would be like, 'Man, you must mean North Korea, 'cause that South Korea, that's one boss fuckin' place'. (It was the 1960s at the time.) But now, I really don't know, South Korea. I think you need to rethink your relationship with the puppy.

I'm not even going to say anything to these puppies. They know what they did.

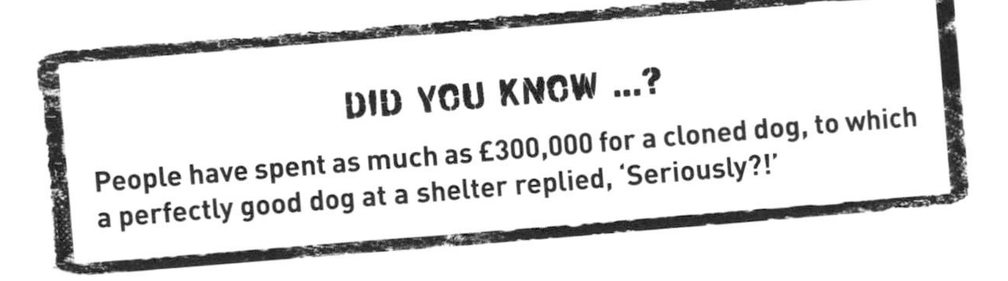

Platypus: the ultimate buzz kill

Nicole Duplaix / NATIONAL GEOGRAPHIC IMAGE COLLECTION / Getty Images

What. The. Fuck. I don't even know what to say, Platypus. YOU MAKE NO SENSE. You're like some kind of anti-drug message, designed to make high people totally freak the fuck out. You are so weird, Platypus, that they don't even have a universally agreed-upon word for the plural form of you. That's because if you see two of these animals together, the fabric of space and time will literally tear apart. Remind me to never close my eyes again, Platypus, you duck-billed asshole.

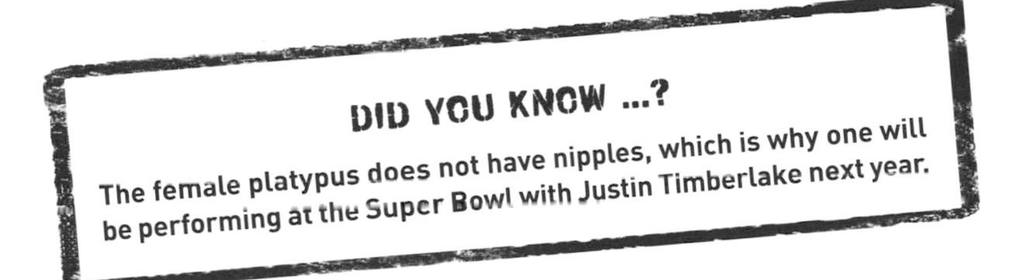

Get a load of this wanker

Craig Dingle / Shutterstock Images LLC

Holy shit, Koala. I didn't realize you were POSING FOR A FUCKING ALBUM COVER FROM THE 1980s. I bet all the songs would be about eucalyptus, seeing as that's all you can eat, you non-omnivorous little shit. Why don't you get down off your tree trunk and act like a normal animal, or are you too good for us? Get lost, Koala. My mind didn't even want to comprehend your cute little existence anyway.

Keep it in your pants, buddy

Eky Chan / Shutterstock Images LLC

You know, Peacock, you are basically a flasher that walks around showing off your stuff to the entire world. It's pretty disgusting, if you ask me, 'beautiful' colours or not. I'm not sure how you decided that you get a free pass from society, but the rest of us have to use our personalities and regular good looks to find mates, instead of throwing our junk around until someone feels sorry for us. Yeah, 'one yes is all it takes', but remember, you have to live with yourself in the morning.

And, yeah, I looked. I'm comfortable with my sexuality, so I can admire a peacock's feathers. THAT DOESN'T MEAN I WANT THEM IN MY FACE ALL DAY, PEACOCK. So either learn to control yourself, or expect to have a sexual harassment suit on your hands.

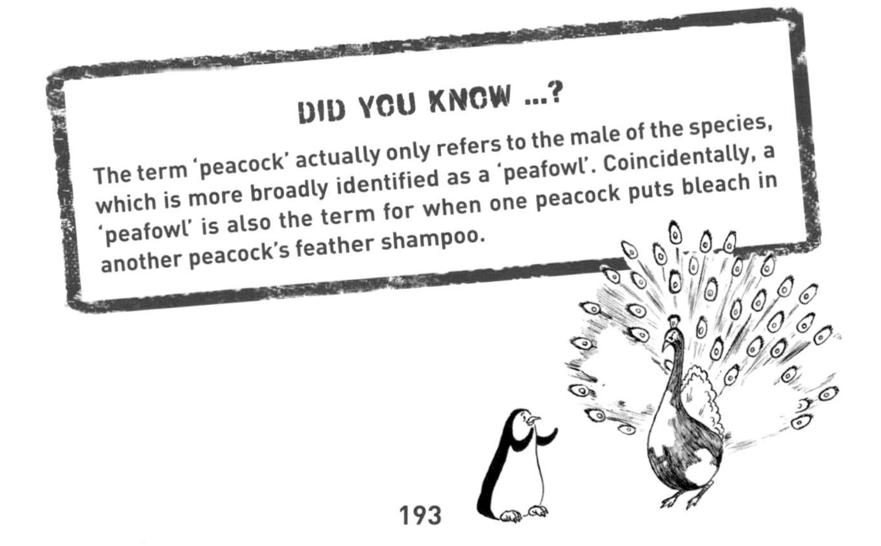

Moles have lowered expectations

Tramper / Shutterstock Images LLC

Oh, hooray, Mole. You made it out of the ground. Why are you so excited? DO YOU WANT A FUCKING MEDAL? Pretty pathetic. First of all, you are a mole; it's kind of like a dolphin being impressed it can swim. And, second, being blind doesn't count as a disability in moles. Maybe if you were driving or operating heavy machinery the look of pride and joy on your face at the moment would be understandable. But at this point, this is standard meat-and-potatoes mole stuff, dude. So just because you're making me share in your joy doesn't mean I'm going to let you get away with it. I'd stay underground until I had a clear life plan moving forward if I were you, Mole.

And, please, nail clippers. They are, like, 50p. Don't tell me you're too lazy to use a shovel.

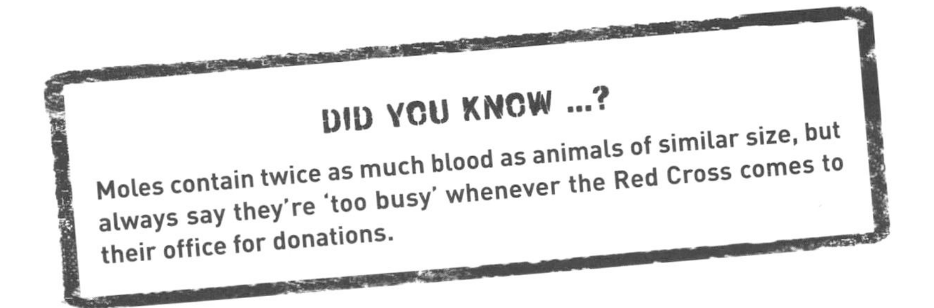

Gazelles are in the pocket of Big Nature Photography

Anke Van Wyk / Shutterstock Images LLC

Here's how this thing went down: The gazelles were hanging out, and the *National Geographic* people came up and said, 'Hey, would you care to make a little money, maybe make a name for yourself?' I'm sure at one point, they said something along the lines of 'Just don't make us look too majestic or spiritual', but let's be honest, they were getting paid so much that they weren't even paying attention when the photographer asked them to stand like that.

Why does everything have to be about the mystical beauty of nature with you? IT LOOKS LIKE YOUR EYES ARE FROM ONE FACE. I really don't have the time or the money to go on an African safari right now, so you need to start acting a little more Korbel and a little less Dom Pérignon. Is it so hard to get by in the African plains on just grass and your integrity? I hope you can sleep at night, gazelles.

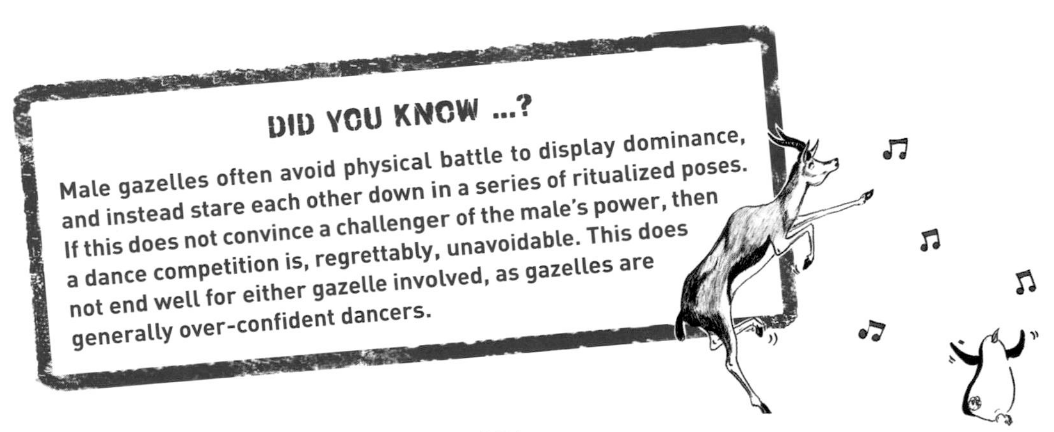

DID YOU KNOW ...?

Male gazelles often avoid physical battle to display dominance, and instead stare each other down in a series of ritualized poses. If this does not convince a challenger of the male's power, then a dance competition is, regrettably, unavoidable. This does not end well for either gazelle involved, as gazelles are generally over-confident dancers.

Puffin hoax revealed!

Leksele / Shutterstock Images LLC

Leksele / Shutterstock Images LLC

There's nothing more obnoxious than a fake animal that tries to pass itself off as an authentic member of the animal world. Puffins are maybe the biggest offenders when it comes to this, even going so far as to pretend to take pictures with humans and hang out in places like Iceland, where no normal person can confirm that they were really there. (Like Iceland is a real place, anyway. Björk is from there!) This photo on the left is a perfect example of the kind of bullshit 'proof' they try to foist on the unsuspecting public. But through some key inside connections, I have obtained an early work print of this photo, displayed on the right, before the puffin had finished its insertion into the real world. IF YOU'RE SO REAL, PUFFIN, WHY DO YOU NEED TO CGI YOUR ASS? Busted, Puffin. Now go back to living inside a fucking eight-year-old girl's head.

I don't approve of you, either

Stephan Kerkhofs / Shutterstock Images LLC

I know you don't like me, Sea Turtle. I can tell not only because of that look plastered across your face, but because you sent me that report card that had 'Needs Improvement' marked all the way down the list. Well, guess what, Sea Turtle? I DON'T THINK YOU'RE SO FUCKING GREAT, EITHER. All you do is live underwater, where you can't breathe, and then come to my beach and bury your eggs all over the place. No one thinks you're better than a tortoise, Sea Turtle, so stop thinking you can judge everyone just because I followed you around the tank at the aquarium for an hour and a half.

Yes, perhaps at one point I may have said something to the effect of 'If only a sea turtle would like me, I could be happy', possibly during a deposition. And it's possible I wanted to have flippers like yours, but knowing how much of a dick I would turn into, I think I'm going to ride this opposable thumb thing out. You see, Turtle (pun intended, fucker), I like my life. Could I change a few things? Sure. But I'll be damned if I'm going to let a sea turtle come over here and tell me how to live.

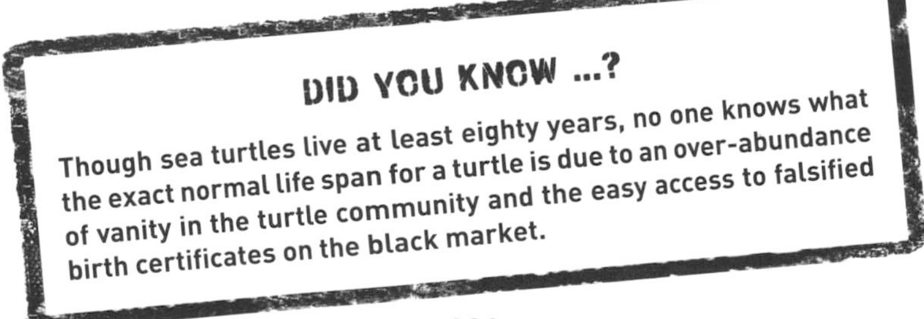

Sloth bears are desperate for attention

Stacey Bates / Shutterstock Images LLC

There's a strict hierarchy when it comes to which bears get attention. Polar bears are at the top of the list because they know people in high places. Panda bears are next because they traded in their sense of dignity in exchange for looking like a teddy bear. Then come grizzly, black and spectacled bears. By the time sloth bears come around, there isn't much left – maybe a tossed-out 'Aww' or a 'Look at the long claws!', but really that's it. Sloth bears are pretty upset about this, especially considering they put a lot of thought into their name, which combines two animals that have a very strong following.

That's where this piece of work comes into the picture. Just back from the salon, Fluffy McPermsalot over here thinks he's going to jump to the front of the line just by doing his hair and striking a cute little bear pose. And you know, maybe I do love his little paws. And yeah, maybe the patch of tan fur around his neck really ties the whole presentation together. But you know what, Sloth Bear? I smell something. Something awful. IT'S THE SMELL OF DESPERATION, BIG GUY, AND IT'S COMING FROM YOU. So until you are ready to love yourself, don't expect anyone to love you back.

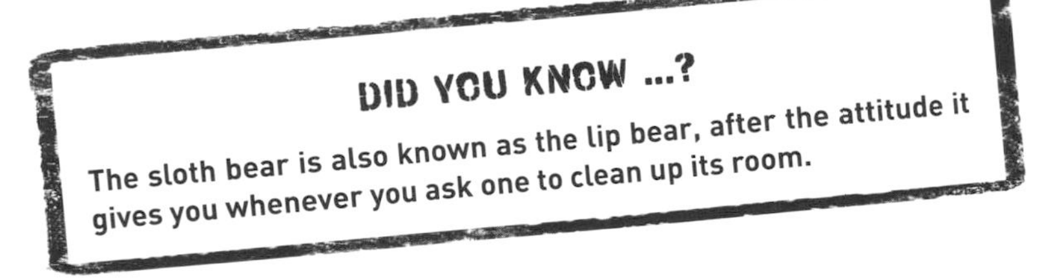

Camels are played out

Mlenny Photography / iStockphoto LP

Come on, Camel. We both know those aren't real, so why don't you get that fucking smirk off your face, stop fucking with everyone and take off those bizarre humps. Yeah, I know you think it's funny, and maybe it was for the first hundred years. Now it's just getting lame. Seriously, Camel, you might as well go around using words like 'bling' and writing articles about metrosexuals and cougars. WELCOME TO 2009, CAMEL. Like you aren't weird-looking enough anyway, Jesus Christ.

Jaded hipster owls think they've seen it all

Lori Skelton / Shutterstock Images LLC

Owls are always making snarky fucking asides like they're above it all. A perfect example of this was the other day. We were eating some really good watermelon sorbet together, and I was like, 'Is this great or what?', and this owl gave me this look and said, 'What'. The fucked-up thing about it was that it was some seriously good watermelon sorbet, too, so there's no way he wasn't enjoying that shit.

So I was all, 'I should already expect it from owls, but you're a real piece of work even for your species, with the curved beak and the silent judging. Sorry, I'm just a person and you get to be inherently wise just because you can turn your head around to look behind your shoulders, Owl. IT'S NOT A CRIME TO OPEN YOURSELF UP TO NEW EXPERIENCES, ASSHOLE.' Then they made me leave the ice-cream store, which was fine with me because there were owl pellets everywhere and that has to be a health violation.

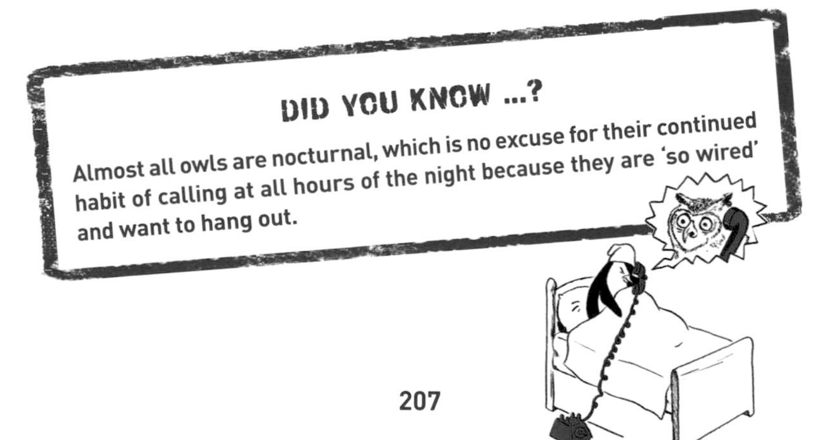

Ugly Animals

We're On To You

Some animals think they can get away with making us want to take a day trip through wine country with them by being incredibly unattractive. This is achieved by being so far up on the ugly scale as to come back around to cute. It's important to let animals know that this is a bullshit move. Just because an animal has a weird nose or is unusually fat in all the wrong places doesn't mean it's off the hook for aggressively ruining my day.

The following are a few of the biggest offenders, but the really messed up part of this aspect of animal cuteness is that any animal is a potential offender. I've seen bats and even fish that have crossed over into ugly cute territory, and they do it with a cockiness that is totally unrelated to their appearance, like that weird guy you know at work. Keep an eye on these dirtbags, because they will get you when you least expect it.

Manatees think they can get away with it

A Cotton Photo / Shutterstock Images LLC

I'm on to you, Manatee. Just because you are arguably the ugliest animal on the planet does not allow you to be so GODDAMNED cute. You are like a pile of flesh that has been twisted into something resembling a normal creature, like a balloon animal that swims.

And what's with the stubby fins and the giant nose? That's just wrong, Manatee. And lose some weight, for crying out loud. You look like a sea cow. STOP LOOKING AT ME LIKE THAT.

Check out Kenny G over here

Alperium / Shutterstock Images LLC

Oh, wow, stellar performance there, hotshot. I forgot how people are always saying, 'You have got to go to the aquarium to hear the music; they are really tearing shit up over there'. Next stop, Covent Garden, right? Okay now, don't even tell me you think you can play saxophone, Walrus. Last time I checked you needed distinguishable digits to use the keys, asshole.

And, dude, you have got to calm down a little bit. You might want to stay for the rest of the show. Do you see dolphins or whales playing instruments? No, they just jump up out of the ocean and get fish. Instant gratification, Walrus. No need to act like the ugly girl; you have a moustache and little tusks. You are hilarious! I mean, Jesus Christ, Walrus, INSTEAD OF HANDS YOU HAVE FLIPPERS. Start respecting yourself, and people will start respecting you.

OH, SNAP!

Hey, Walrus, yo mama's so ugly, she only manages to get pregnant once every two years!

The follies of youth

Pigeons are cool. They leave me alone, shit on ugly statues and almost never mug for the camera. During war, they do their duty and carry messages from place to place. All in all, pigeons are like the beat-up pickup truck of the animal world. Nothing pretty, but they get the job done.

Baby pigeons, on the other hand, are fucking assholes. Look at this little shit, with his crooked beak and skin that looks like a withered scrotum. I'm sorry, did you take the threads from a corncob and rub them all over your body? You're lucky you grow up to be all business, Baby Pigeon, because that shit is just fucking adorable, and that is a serious problem. I'm going to give you a pass now, because you have a right to get your jollies out a little during your formative years, but I *swear*, Baby Pigeon, if you still look this cute once you join the pigeon workforce, I WILL NOT BE SO FORGIVING.

OH, SNAP!

Hey, Pigeon, yo mama's so ugly she wasn't allowed to leave her nest until she was two months old!

What the fuck are you looking at?

Jeff R. Chow / Shutterstock Images LLC

I see you eyeing me, Armadillo, and I have to say I don't care for it. It's not that weird for me to be interested. YOU ARE AN ARMADILLO IN A BUCKET. Did you think this kind of thing would go unchallenged? The truth of the matter is that armadillos should never be in buckets. We've all seen you out there rolling yourself into a ball, digging holes and dancing on the Internet. An armadillo has to do what an armadillo has to do. But there's no reason you should pop out of that bucket, with your little nose and your big ears and those paws, and give me a big stink eye, like, 'Yeah, that's right, I'm an armadillo, and I'm inside your fucking bucket'. All I have to say is that you better get right out of that bucket, Armadillo, and get the HELL out of my face. Your days of weird-looking intimidation are semi-over, Armadillo.

Turkeys need to practise more

Christopher Elwell / Shutterstock Images LLC

The head tilt? Really, Turkey? I can't believe you think you can just waltz over here and toss me a head tilt and call it a day. It's not like you are a puppy or a bear or something. You have weird growths all over your neck and your head is almost totally bald. YOU NEED TO TAKE BETTER CARE OF YOURSELF, TURKEY. Give me something I can use, like standing on one leg while juggling, or becoming friends with a pig and sleeping with your wing around it. The head tilt is just lazy, Turkey.

Look, I get it, you're a turkey, you've got other things on your mind. I wouldn't want to be associated with a major American holiday that focuses almost exclusively on food, either. But the best way to turn the tide on the whole Thanksgiving thing is to get inside the minds of these people. Now, I'm not advocating any kind of cuteness campaign; that would be against everything I stand for here at Fuck You, Penguin. *But if I were*, I would tell you one thing: less neck, more butt. Now get to work, you miserable bastard.

Don't listen to groundhogs

Alan Freed / Shutterstock Images LLC

I know your secret, Groundhog. You've had a free ride for way too long. News flash: Groundhogs do not know how to predict the weather. It was inevitable that people would start to catch on, since you have to switch it up every now and then to keep them guessing, but every year the spring continues to arrive at the same time. You've only been able to last this long because of the teeth, Groundhog, those damn teeth, taunting me with their prominence. But those teeth cannot save you for long, because if you don't put them away, I am definitely going to see my shadow. And then it's going to be a long, cold winter for you, Groundhog. And it's going to last you the rest of your life.

Tarsiers are corporate shills

iNNOCENt / Shutterstock Images LLC

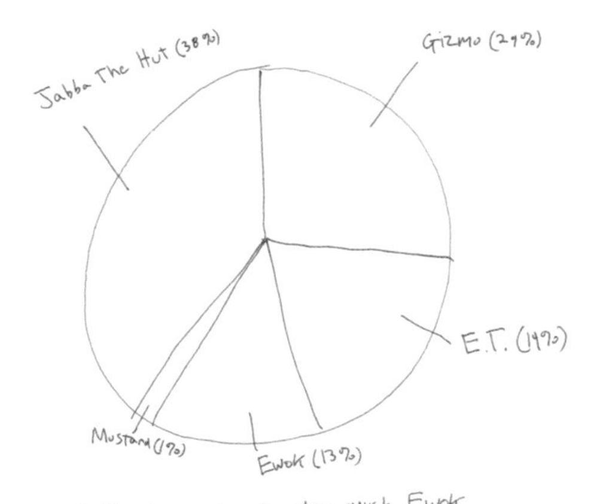

Chart provided by J. Wass at The Fake Institute (TFI)

While it may seem like tarsiers are prosimian primates of the genus Tarsius that are currently found in the islands of Southeast Asia, they are actually a heavily focus-grouped product designed to bring ugly animals into the twenty-first century. Created from a synthesis of well-known movie aliens (see the chart opposite), the tarsier is one of the craziest-looking motherfuckers ever, but for some odd reason I can't help but want to have a deep conversation with it about where it comes from and whether or not I can go back there with it.

As you can tell from this sneaky one right here, that is precisely the plan for these unstoppable marketing forces. The fact that this wanker can half-close one eye while keeping the other wide open only confirms that he is not content to rest on his disgustingly furry laurels. But I know better, Tarsier. I expect a little heart from my ugly animals. Next time, a little more Chewie, a little less Jar Jar.

Hippo charm is a fucking joke

Eclectic Fishbowl / iStockphoto LP

Don't be coy, you fucking semi-aquatic jerk. Your dashing good looks and slightly tilted head are not going to work on me. Are you actually kissing the ground, Hippo? That is not hygienic in any way, and I'm pretty sure there is literally no animal on the planet, hippo or not, that would find that attractive. The only other option is that your head is just too fucking enormous for your body, in which case I totally get it, because it totally is. And what's with the pose for the camera? Are you in a beauty pageant or something? 'Cause I got news for you: THE ZEBRA IS GOING TO KICK YOUR ASS. Stay humble, Hippo. No one likes a show-off.

Fuck You, Penguin

The Early Years

Earlier this year, I received a fake letter from a person that I made up which really moved me. In it, I wrote, 'Dear Fuck You, Penguin, You are the most wonderful person in the world, but more importantly, you are so effective and naturally gifted at putting animals in their place! How is it possible for other people to live their lives as honourably as you when we do not have the same God-given talents?'

I thought this was really well put, but the truth is that the transition from Cute Victim to Cute Repeller did not come easily, even for me. In fact, anyone who decides to no longer let cute animals rule their life must work at it every day. To help you get through this process, I have included a few of my early instalments of Fuck You, Penguin, before I was able to free myself from the chains that bound me. Because these are such important documents, anyone reading this who works at the Smithsonian can email me at fupenguin@gmail.com about adding these to the collection, but, please, don't embarrass me by offering too much money. I'm just happy to help my country.

Irish wolfhounds make me want to murder

Brian Weed / Shutterstock Images LLC

Early correspondence from my dark period:

FROM THE DESK OF FUCK YOU, PENGUIN

Dear Lady,
You seem like a very nice lady, with your scarf and your model release form. So please do not take this the wrong way, but I want to come to your house, tie you up and steal your dog. We (your dog and I) will then proceed to go on a killing and bank-robbing spree à la Bonnie and Clyde, which will result in both of us being showered in a downpour of bullets, preferably to that Hawaiian guy's version of 'What a Wonderful World'.

Sincerely,
Fuck You, Penguin

Thank you to the Federal Bureau of Investigation for permission to use this letter in the book.

Who's a kitten?

Tony Campbell / Shutterstock Images LLC

Oh man, what a cute kitten playing in the grass! What are you doing in the grass, Kitten? Whoos uh wuvvy widdle kitten? You are! That's right! YES YOU ARE.

Wait a second. Get it together. Breathe. Okay. Okay, let's do this thing. Yeah. YEAH. HEY, KITTEN, YOU SUCK. Yeah, that'll show him. Now I'm coming in for the big one: FUUUU ... GOSHDARNIT, KITTEN. You are so cute, I mean, shhhh ... dagnabbit!

I didn't mean it, Kitten. I'm sorry. Just go back to playing in the grass. You can stand on your hind legs whenever you want. Forgive me for using such harsh language around your delicate ears. Would you like any milk? Okay, well, just let me know.

I hung out with this panda!!!!!!

Kitch Bain / Shutterstock Images LLC

Okay, so are we ready to do this thing? You don't have to do anything, just stand there like that, you're looking great. Well, maybe you could put your cute little paw on the ledge there, I mean, only if you want to ... Okay, great, wow, you really are the consummate professional, aren't you? It's a real honour to work with you. Okay, ready:

Hey, Panda, FUCK YOU. That's right, you heard me. Stop being so clumsy and cute, or I'm gonna ARRRRRRR!!!!! [Shakes fist.]

Okay, that should do it. Great to work with you, really, an honour. Hey, I know you are pretty busy, but would you mind signing this? It's for my son. Just make it out to FUP, he doesn't like being called by his name. Thanks, this was really great. Hey, if you want to grab something to eat, I was just going over to a great bamboo patch I know ... Okay, that's cool, I know you've got some meetings and stuff, no worries, okay, see you around.

Newfie pups don't phase this motherfucker

Daniel Gale / Shutterstock Images LLC

You fucking bastard. Why can't both of your eyes be the same size? I'm on to you, Puppy. You can't stop me. Stay out of my way, you goddamned asshole. And if you EVER put your chin on ANYTHING again, so help me, Puppy, so fucking help me ...

Daniel Gale / Shutterstock Images LLC

Daniel Gale / Shutterstock Images LLC

Daniel Gale / Shutterstock Images LLC; inhaus creative / iStockphoto LP

Dear Puppy,

I'm really sorry about this. Have you been avoiding chin resting because of me? I didn't actually mean what I said, I swear. In order to show you that I really don't mind if you put your chin on anything (honest), I've Photoshopped you onto various things on which you can (should?!) rest your chin.

I hope you can forgive me.

Sincerely,
Fuck You, Penguin

Acknowledgements

A book like this requires an enormous amount of effort from me, and then a little bit of effort from a bunch of different people. The person who probably deserves that joke least is my editor, Danielle Perez, who loved the blog from the first moment she heard about it and never stopped being extremely supportive, even when she was astutely pointing out all the stuff in the first draft that I already kind of knew wasn't funny enough yet. I also want to thank my agent, Daniel Greenberg, who saw the book potential earlier than even I did, and helped me through the process with amazing patience for my ignorance and an impressive lack of expressiveness in his voice. Thank you as well to my UK editor, Victoria McGeown, and Emily Flake, who created the amazing illustrations for this edition.

Then there are the people who really make this book what it is: the photographers, amateur and professional alike, who captured their subjects at the best (worst) moments possible, and the people who helped me get in contact with them. Thank you to Claire Bartholome, Roni and John Seabury, A.J. Maher, Kem Sypher, Paul Sweedlund, Lauren Billings, Seattle Roll, John Vermilye, Luiz Marigo, Carrie, Vicki Jedlicka, Kathrin Gaisser, Surinder Singh, Derek White, Jerry Weinstein, Kevin Schafer, Jeff Jeffords, Sean and Kelly SosikHamor, Adrian Pingstone, Milo Burcham, Vassil, Rachel Otty, Crystal McKay, Joy Zaczyk, Rebekah Winkler, Denise Martinez Alanis, Tony and Amy Pardo, Deena Lang, Katie Owen, Matt Greenwood, Zach Walker and Angela Hamilton.

Thank you to all the readers who forwarded the blog and all of the regular commenters who make the site even stranger than it already is. Thanks in particular to Dianne McGunigle, who found the blog through some kind of magic she refuses to reveal for fear of the public misunderstanding her power. She's most likely the biggest reason you are holding this book today. And a special thank you to David Christian, Julian Wass, Sarah and Dan Blank, Adrian Covert and Dan Lopez, who helped me with the technical stuff that I'm too incompetent to do myself. Finally, thank you to my wife, Audrey, the only person who can hurt my feelings by telling me something I wrote isn't funny enough, and the woman who once again proves that in front of every great man trying to make something happen, there's a far greater woman being too awesome and getting everyone's attention.